UFOs & UFO Secrets— Area 51, Alien & UFO Encounters, Alien Civilizations & the New World Order

© **Copyright 2015 Alex Monaldo - All rights reserved.**

In no way is it legal to reproduce, duplicate, or transmit any part of this document in either electronic means or in printed format. Recording of this publication is strictly prohibited and any storage of this document is not allowed unless with written permission from the publisher. All rights reserved.

The information provided herein is stated to be truthful and consistent, in that any liability, in terms of inattention or otherwise, by any usage or abuse of any policies, processes, or directions contained within is the solitary and utter responsibility of the recipient reader. Under no circumstances will any legal responsibility or blame be held against the publisher for any reparation, damages, or monetary loss due to the information herein, either directly or indirectly.
Respective authors own all copyrights not held by the publisher.

Legal Notice:
This book is copyright protected. This is only for personal use. You cannot amend, distribute, sell, use, quote or paraphrase any part or the content within this book without the consent of the author or copyright owner. Legal action will be pursued if this is breached.

Disclaimer Notice:
Please note the information contained within this document is for educational and entertainment purposes only. Every attempt has been made to provide accurate, up to date and reliable complete information. No warranties of any kind are expressed or implied. Readers acknowledge that the author is

not engaging in the rendering of legal, financial, medical or professional advice.

By reading this document, the reader agrees that under no circumstances are we responsible for any losses, direct or indirect, which are incurred as a result of the use of information contained within this document, including, but not limited to, —errors, omissions, or inaccuracies.

Table of Contents

Introduction 5

Chapter 1 – Do You Believe in Aliens? The Mystery of Extraterrestrial Life Forms.. 12

Chapter 2 – Aliens Among Us – Extraterrestrial Imagery in Pop Culture 17

Chapter 3 – The Roswell UFO Incident 26

Chapter 4 – The Secrets of Area 51 31

Chapter 5 – Alien Encounters, Abductions, and UFO Sightings 41

Chapter 6 – Testimonies and Stories.. 45

Chapter 7 – Alien Civilizations & The New World Order and the Majestic 12.. 66

Chapter 8 – Ancient Aliens 75

Chapter 9 – Religion and Aliens.. 80

Chapter 10 – Unconfirmed Evidence 99

Chapter 11 – What Makes the United States of America so Special? 109

Chapter 12 – Rare Natural Phenomena, Aliens, or Something Else? 119

Chapter 13 – Alien & UFO Fun Facts... 130

Chapter 14 – The Latest Alien and UFO News 135

Best Practices and Common Mistakes 139

Conclusion... 141

Introduction

PROBABLY THE BEST BOOK CLUB ONLINE...
"If you love books. You will love the Lean Stone Book Club"

*** **Exclusive Deals** That *Any* Book Fan Would Love! ***

Visit leanstonebookclub.com/join

(IT'S FREE)!

Aliens and life on other planets have always been a subject of fascination for a lot of people and the topic of heated debate. Are aliens real? Are they just the figment of our collective imagination? What about the people who claim to have seen them or to have been abducted by them? Are they "chosen ones" or merely hallucinating? The topic lends itself to wild speculations, precisely because it's something we know next to nothing about. We have never had an officially confirmed sight, encounter or sign of alien existence. Since their presence has never been confirmed, you could easily assume they're a myth, like leprechauns or unicorns.

But it's not that simple. There is no reason that aliens shouldn't exist. In fact, no matter what theory of creation you ascribe to – either intelligent design or evolution – it would be logical for other life forms to exist in the vast outer space. So, if we believe they do exist, that only leaves us to establish contact or, at least, confirm a sighting or a sign of some sort. Alas, despite thousands of claims over the years, that has never been possible. Is that because they were proven to be false, or because someone doesn't *want* us to know?

There is so much secrecy surrounding the topic of aliens that it's hard not to get sucked into the rabbit hole of conspiracy theories. That doesn't mean that we should all start manufacturing tinfoil hats, but all this mystery does make you wonder, doesn't it? If aliens exist and we have confirmed evidence, then why don't we know about it? If they don't exist, then why won't anyone come out and say it outright? And what about all the people who have reported sightings? Something isn't right about this, and we are right to be suspicious. Someone somewhere is hiding something; that we know for sure. But why? Perhaps that is the question that is more important.

What do you think? Are we secretly being visited by our neighbors from other planets? Are they studying us, planning for a future invasion? Or are you among the skeptics who completely rule out this possibility. Most likely, you are not sure what to think; I mean, the evidence is there, but not really. It's easy to be torn on this issue because we have no conclusive evidence in either direction. So then, what do you believe? Perhaps it would be easier for you to form an opinion if you had all the facts.

Well, that's exactly what this book is for. This book was written mainly for the people who are unsure about what to believe, regarding alien life forms. All the major and most important facts, stories, and conspiracy theories are detailed in this guide to aliens and UFOs. If you've always been curious about them but didn't know where to start, this book is a great place to begin your journey into the secret relationship between aliens and humans. Is it real or is it just fiction? You be the one to judge.

And to do that, there are some things we need to clear up, first and foremost – there are certain preconceived ideas that people have about aliens and individuals who study or believe in alien life forms. Before you dive into the book, I would like to ask you to take a few moments to read this next section in which I address a few of these common misconceptions that are insulting and damaging to people who are interested in UFOs.

Common misconceptions about UFOs, aliens and the people who believe in them:

- **Individuals who believe in aliens are unintelligent.**

If you are over the age of 12, and you think that or, worse, say that to people's faces, then I am sorry for you. Believing that aliens exist cannot, by any stretch of the imagination, be called stupid. First of all, the evidence is not conclusive in either direction, so you cannot make a judgment call and say, for a fact, that extraterrestrial life forms do or do not exist. Secondly, if everyone had this attitude, we wouldn't be studying, researching or discovering anything, because of plenty of things "obviously" don't exist, so what's the point?

Look, I see where you're coming from – you think that if there is no substantial evidence behind it, believing that aliens exist is misguided and silly. But reflect on the fact that people once thought the Earth was flat, that there were no continents left to discover or that the Sun revolved around the Earth, instead of the other way around. We sent men to the moon, for God's sake! Few things are actually outside the realm of possibility, so keep an open mind.

- **People who claim to have seen or met aliens are lying.**

We don't know for sure what these people experienced because we weren't there. Of course, there is a very high possibility that they are lying for attention or that they sincerely believe to have been abducted, for example, when they were not, but the same possibility exists for their stories to be true. Unless they can be disproven without a doubt, we can't actually rule out their claims, can we? There have been cases of witnesses that were proven to be false, but there are also still a lot of cases that are left unknown.

- **Christians can't believe in the existence of extraterrestrials.**

I hear this argument often, and I don't really understand it, to be honest. Entertaining the idea that there might be life on other planets does not mean that anyone is worshipping some other form of life. These are not gods, they are other civilizations; like alternative humans, if you will. And in all fairness, the argument for the existence of aliens is stronger on the religious side than on the non-religious one.

Think about it – would an intelligent creator have made an entire, endless, ever-expanding universe if they didn't intend to populate it? Why only make humans on Earth? Why create such comparatively insignificant life on a small planet in one corner of the universe, when there is so much more out there? It really makes you think about the things we *believe that* we know for sure, but know next to nothing about. After all, the universe is still a mystery.

You see, the fascination is contagious, and it's hard not to become curious. I don't think I know a single soul who holds a genuinely neutral opinion on the subject. Some may believe that they do, but they are much more involved than they realize. It's one of those polarizing topics that divide people on one side or the other, with few to no exception. That may seem baffling because, at the end of the day, it's not something that affects us directly, does it? Life goes on, and the Earth revolves the same way it has for billions of years. So, then why are we so committed to this narrative?

Because it's one of life's great mysteries. Right up there with the existence of God, the afterlife, and the meaning of life on Earth, the existence of extraterrestrials is something that fascinates us and interests us deeply. And for the sake of this fascination, we struggle to understand these concepts we may not be entirely familiar with. But how can we begin to understand aliens and UFOs?

Well, a good place to start is to look at the etymology of these very terms. What do they mean? Where do they come from? Who coined this term and what were they supposed to represent?

- **UFO** – An Unidentified Flying Object or a UFO, as it is most commonly referred to, is an object or phenomenon one might notice in the sky, but not be able to place it, explain it or identify it. The term originated in the United States Air Force (or the USAF), which created the concept as a way of labeling all sightings of this kind. When it first emerged, the term was deemed by the USAF as: "any airborne object which by performance, aerodynamic characteristics, or unusual features, does not conform to any presently known aircraft or missile type, or which cannot be positively identified as a familiar object." This is how it was defined in the Air Force Regulation 200-2.

Prior to the emergence of the term UFO, these objects were known as flying saucers or flying discs, which were both popular terms. However, Unidentified Flying Object was popularized as a label especially in the Cold War, when national security was believed to be threatened in more ways than one. An alien invasion seemed like a stronger possibility than ever before, despite numerous studies that have since shown that the appearance of so-called UFOs was never a threat at the time, and they do not pose a threat now.

- **Alien** – An alien, often also called "space alien," in order to differentiate it from the legal term of "alien," is generally a word used to describe an extraterrestrial being. According to popular culture, aliens are supposedly of a much higher intelligence than humans and keepers of incredible technology, information, and secrets of the universe. In the scientific sense, aliens can be bacteria or other minor or undeveloped organisms, but most commonly, they are known as vaguely humanoid beings that live in outer space and who may or may not be interested in invading Earth and/or conducting tests on humans.

  As far as appearance goes, the extraterrestrial being has no "official" form, since no life forms have ever been discovered. However, that didn't stop us from dreaming up a few typologies that enjoyed more or less popularity over the years and which were either completely made up or based on the recollections of those who claim to have seen or interacted with aliens. Among these iterations, surely you are familiar with the Greys, the small green men, and the Reptilians, but I will expand upon these later in the book.

Are you curious to find out more about aliens and UFOs? Are you interested in what people have to say? What about the conspiracy theories? Do they hold water, or are they mere paranoid fever dreams? Can anyone know for sure whether aliens exist or not? And how can UFO sightings be explained? If you want to read more about all of these things, stay tuned!

Chapter 1: Do You Believe In Aliens? The Mystery of Extraterrestrial Life Forms

In this chapter, you will learn:

- What aliens are and what we understand by the term
- How the concept of aliens developed and influenced our society

Aliens, by definition, are life forms that exist on other planets outside Earth. Also, known as extraterrestrials, you are surely familiar with these somewhat modern mythological creatures or urban legends. The question of whether life exists on other planets or not isn't a novel one, by any means. In fact, appeared as soon as humans discovered the existence of other planets within the solar system.

If humans inhabit the Earth, then the presence of other planets begs the question "Are other *humans* living on other planets?" Even though that question first appeared in the minds of humans' centuries ago, we still do not hold the answer, which makes it one of the biggest mysteries of the world we live in.

Logical conclusions vs. lack of proof

The paradox about extraterrestrials is that some scientists are relatively sure they exist. In theory. You see, if we consider the way the universe is formed, there is no reason to assume that other life forms do not exist on other planets. In fact, one could argue it is almost impossible, or, at least, improbable, for all other planets (within our solar system or outside it) to be barren except for Earth.

However, what we lack, at least at this moment, is proof. Well, Mars presents signs of possible life forms and water, but we don't yet know how conclusive that evidence is. And until we are able to study those traces up close, it is difficult to know for sure what they are, what caused them and how long ago.

We didn't really look into it before the mid-20th century, when the study of extraterrestrial life forms, how likely they were to exist and under what form really boomed. That is also when aliens entered popular culture in full force and brought with it a surge in UFO sightings. Suddenly, everyone was interested in alien life forms. Did aliens exist? What did they look like? Did they visit Earth and what did they want from us?

Aliens among us

It is intriguing, without a doubt. For so long, we have had this sincerely held belief that we, alone, populate the universe because there was no evidence to the contrary. Entertaining the idea that we might have small, green, big-eyed company is revolutionary, to say the least. What does this mean for our civilization? Have we already had encounters we don't know about? Have aliens influenced our society or development in ways we cannot even begin to imagine? Or is this whole thing just beginning?

There are just too many variables to consider, and the lack of a definite response definitely fuels the suppositions, stories, scenarios and conspiracy theories. Who's to say that someone has or has not had genuine encounters with aliens? Actually, there are quite a few people who ascribe to the belief that aliens are already among us. That theory has been particularly popular in the 90s, and it was brought up more than once that aliens might be already walking the Earth, without our knowledge! There was a time when people would be suspicious of each other and suspect each other of being alien life forms, based on weird or unfamiliar behavior.

Obviously, that is a dangerous precedent, because it takes the concept of "othering" to new extremes that have never been reached before. Just because a person is displaying a type of behavior that is perceived as uncommon by the mainstream, it doesn't mean that a) there is anything wrong with them, b) you have the right to treat them as lesser beings or c) they are not human. I think we can agree that is preposterous. However, it stands as the ultimate proof that if you plant the seed of fear in people and you repeat the same fear-mongering ideas over and over, paranoia will install itself in the minds of even the most logical and level-headed of people. None of us are immune.

Considering extensive study

Of course, there are thousands upon thousands of pages of literature, scientific study and other materials worth reading on the subject, and I strongly recommend you expand your research further and give other sources a read. Not only because it will make it significantly easier for you to make an informed decision on whether or not you actually believe in extraterrestrial existence, but because the subject is endlessly fascinating.

It is impossible to cover every aspect of the alien controversy in this book, which is why I urge you to continue to read about it even after you finish this book. Hopefully, it will open your appetite for deeper research and discovery and who knows? Maybe you could even stumble upon some answers to your burning questions. Especially when it comes to scientific explanations, it is imperative for you to check out something backed up by NASA or a similarly established organization, as a) I do not possess the authority to make claims on the matter and b) this book focuses more on the controversy and conspiracy theories, rather than the actual research conducted in this area.

Do you believe in aliens?

So, then, what do you think? Apparently, you cannot form an opinion based on just the limited information presented here. There is a world of facts out there, and you have to take that into consideration. But like any kind of belief, this is a gut thing, more than anything else. Some people are born skeptics, and they will die, skeptics, while others really want to believe, whether it's aliens, superstitions or tarot cards. In a world where nothing is certain, and we find out new things about ourselves, our human nature, our origins and our planet every single day, who can say that they know for sure if we are alone in the universe or not?

Looking at both sides of the coin, believing that aliens exist makes as much sense as not believing they do. There is no judgment – at least in this space, we've created here – on either side, no matter where you land on. Perhaps your mind is already made up, and you know exactly what you think and what you believe. You, my friend, are one of the lucky ones because few people are confident in their beliefs. If, however, you are still open to new information and interpretations, then please go ahead and read the rest of the book so that you can form a complete and accurate impression of the fascinating aspects of UFOs, extraterrestrial beings and their influence on us earthlings.

As for me, I can't pick a side. I am personally completely open to both sides of the issue, and I am eager to receive compelling evidence one way or another. I, too, have had moments when I thought I saw something unusual; for days, I was convinced that what I noticed in the sky was actually an alien spacecraft. But then again, I had no evidence, did I? I am endlessly intrigued by the accounts of people who claim to have been abducted and studies by extraterrestrials, and I'm not gonna lie, I wish they are true. But since at this time, we can't know for sure, all we can do is continue to research the matter and inform ourselves further.

Chapter 2: Aliens Among Us – Extraterrestrial Imagery In Pop Culture

In this chapter, you will learn:

- What the most popular alien fiction is
- How aliens have been presented over the years

History, aliens, and pop culture

As you may already know by now, aliens are not a concept that was invented overnight. In fact, the height of the crazy was in the 1940s-1950s, back when UFOs were better known as "flying saucers," because of the ovoid shape they had. Over the course of one century, extraterrestrials went from being an abstract concept to materializing into beings of different forms, sizes, and colors, according to one's imagination or claims. As time went by, they became more and more popular, especially in an America that found itself under threat during the Cold War. Space was, indeed, the final frontier, and there was no knowledge of what this vast unknown could hold.

This great mystery gave birth to some of the most iconic concepts and imagery in pop culture: the aliens, in their many forms and iterations. In fact, suppositions of the existence of life on other planets were made in fiction as early as the 17th century, with descriptions following shortly. Much later, in the 20th century, the popularity of aliens grew in the sci-fi community, thanks to comic books. "Alien" comes to mind as one of the most fruitful and long-standing, having entered the collective consciousness, along with their illustration of extraterrestrials as gray, monster-like beings. The series later had the famous movie franchise "Alien" modeled after it and spawned others, like "Alien vs. Predator".

The "War of the Worlds" hysteria

However, perhaps the singular most famous moment in pop culture history was Orson Welles' rendition of "The War of the Worlds," by H.G. Wells. If you are unfamiliar with the incident, let me tell you a little story. Written at the end of the 19th century, "The War of the Worlds" is a novel by H.G. Welles, depicting a Martian invasion of London. Decades later, it was made into a radio play narrated by Orson Welles, which lead to the infamous incident of 1938. But first, some background information about this piece of fiction.

Aside from the natural curiosity and fascination with the unfamiliar, the possibility of the existence of aliens also sparked a sort of fear in the population. The idea of foreign invaders permeated the collective consciousness and people everywhere were bracing for the alien invasion. You know, similar to how people are now preparing for the zombie apocalypse, but less fictional. This all culminated in the infamous "War of the Worlds" incident, narrated by Orson Welles on the radio.

"The War of the Worlds" is written in the first person, and it is a supposedly factual description of a Martian invasion. Details are abundant, including descriptions of the aliens themselves, said to be "big," "the size [...] of a bear", with "oily brown skin,"

"V-shaped mouths" and "two large dark-colored eyes." They are also described to have tentacles. They are, by all accounts, big, monstrous and menacing, and they are invading the Earth. Now, this detailed account of this invasion from Mars is presented on the radio, in 1938, as a news bulletin. The information is relayed as if it were actually happening.

As the story goes, the show was so believable, that the listeners who tuned in late and didn't catch the fact that this was no more than a play thought that these were facts being relayed on the radio, in an urgent, incredible broadcast. Panic ensued, as people were desperate to escape the alien invasion. Of course, we can't know for sure. Some believe the facts were just exaggerated by the written press, in an effort to discredit the reliability and credibility of radio, while others believe that it was all just a stunt carefully orchestrated by Orson Welles himself.

This incident caused fear and scandal because the concept of such foreign entities was so unfamiliar. People fear the unknown, so the mere idea of these being existing automatically leads to preconceived notions that they are out to invade the Earth, even in the absence of any such indication. Aliens, real or fictional, have tremendous power over people in that they generate strong feelings of either fear or fascination. Sometimes, it's both. That is precisely why they are so present in popular culture and why we have books, movies, comics, TV shows, and even songs ("I'm in love with an alien," anyone?) related to this very subject. People just love talking about aliens, and they love the mystery.

Good aliens, dangerous aliens

But no matter what the truth is, the fact that people believed it as reality is a testament to the very real fear that people subconsciously feel when it comes to the great unknown that is extraterrestrial life. As far as we know, alien invasions (be it Martian or otherwise) are still entirely fictional, and they've been the central plot to decades and dozens of movies. Some of them are more serious and meant to replicate or anticipate, perhaps, a real-life situation, while some are merely spoofs that aim to make light of this improbable scenario.

Over the years, aliens have been depicted as these highly intelligent, but ultimately evil beings. They serve as anti-heroes, if you will, who use their incredible superiority for bad, not good. Instead of helping humanity, they always seek to destroy it, invade it, kidnap it, abduct it, conduct tests on it, harvest its organs, or eggs, etc. In our collective mind, extraterrestrials have, intentionally or not, been associated with malevolent purposes. We don't have warm and fuzzy feelings about these beings who have been portrayed, time and time again, as cold, unfeeling, inhuman, and interested in exploiting our race.

One of the very few counterpoints to that view is the massively successful movie E.T., which influenced and maybe even shaped an entire generation of children's understanding of aliens. Unlike their parents and grandparents, who were taught to fear the unknown coming from outer space during those paranoid and threatening times of the Cold War, these children were presented with a new perspective: this alien was friendly, smart, funny and had human-like characteristics and feelings. I won't give away any spoilers, but it's a tear-jerker.

Different types and their representation

Something to take note of is the fact that with each of these iterations of extraterrestrials came a new kind of appearance for them. Since aliens are not something we know exist, their form was left entirely to our imagination. Thus, we have come up with several kinds of aliens, in varying degrees of scariness, to satisfy our curiosity and our frankly terrifying imagination. Scaly, green, ugly, googly-eyed, with trunks and tentacles or missing noses altogether, aliens are depicted in a lot of different ways.

Aliens are tough to picture because while they would present different characteristics than us, having developed on a different planet and adapted to a very different environment, they are still vaguely humanoid beings and are extremely, dangerously intelligent. Thanks to this combination, people have dreamed up aliens to have our same basic structure (head, limbs, etc.) and facial features, with slight variations caused by adapting to their environment or the redundancy of a characteristic, like ears or noses, for example.

Aliens can come in. However, many shapes and sizes we can imagine; their form depends on our creativity. However, there are a few that have stuck in the public consciousness and which tend to make appearances and reappearances in conspiracy theories, claims of having witnessed their presence and stories of abduction. So, let's dedicate this space to describing a few of the "traditional" aliens, or the most popular ones.

Grays – Perhaps the most "classic" and recognizable of all, the gray aliens are the standard ones we encounter in most movies and cartoons. The grays are humanoid, but they are different. First of all, their skin is dark gray and has a different texture from ours, due to the different atmosphere and lack of sunlight on their home planet. They are smaller than regular humans, but their heads are comparatively huge for the size of their bodies. They are also bald. They lack noses, lips, and ears, instead presenting nostrils and slits in the place of mouths. Their eyes are massive and black and have an elongated almond shape.

Their bodies are similar to ours, except their arms are significantly longer, and they only have 3 to 4 fingers, including an opposable thumb. They also do not present visible genitals; however, there are various accounts from people describing such aliens and claiming that they've had their eggs or sperm harvested or that they were sexually abused by the extraterrestrials, supposedly, for reproduction purposes.

This representation is one of the oldest and most common, and it can be traced back to accounts from the Roswell incident in 1947. After that, people started coming forward with stories of abduction and extraterrestrial interaction that heavily featured these gray beings.

Little green men – The little green men are another form that aliens often take in modern culture and one that you are more than likely familiar with. They are also humanoid beings who are considerably smaller than people and who present the same kind of characteristics as the Grays. Sometimes, they have antennae. This representation may seem modern, but it also dates way back. You may encounter them or remember them from fantastic novels in the 1950s, as well as cartoons. In fact, the 50s is the period when this significantly more harmless characterization of aliens was popularized. Compared to other monstrous representations that I'm going to get to in a moment, these small green men with antennae can even look funny. Shows like "The Flintstones" featured them back in the day, as well as other popular programs for children and adults alike.

Reptilians – Now we're verging into conspiracy theory territory, but I can't overlook mentioning Reptilians, precisely because this is such a popular opinion. The Reptilian theory (also known as Lizard Men) originated somewhere at the beginning of the 20th century in fiction. This kind of extraterrestrial often features in comic books, movies and other forms of sci-fi media, proving to be quite popular. However, some people go beyond the "fiction" part of sci-fi and claim that Reptilians are an evil extraterrestrial civilization that has already overtaken the Earth.

Proponents of this conspiracy theory claim that these creatures have shape-shifting capabilities and that they have successfully exceeded positions of power here on Earth, especially politicians. It has now become fairly common for someone to accuse a public figure of being a secret Reptilian. David Icke, conspiracy theorist par excellence, is convinced that influential figures such as George W. Bush or Queen Elizabeth II are Reptilian leaders. Better yet (let's use "better" loosely), an alleged 4% of American registered voters believed the same as recently as 2013.

Obviously, we have no proof of that, and it would be very hard to attain it, given that Reptilians are supposedly shape-shifters. According to the same Icke, the so-called Lizard People are very tall (ranging from 1.5m to 3.7m), and humanoid in appearance, except for their reptile scales and the fact that they drink blood.

The Alien – In the same terrifying category, there's the extraterrestrial illustrated by the "Alien" series, which is far more menacing-looking than the little green men or even the grays. This creature has claws, a long tail, and an oblong head that end in rows and rows of tremendous, very sharp teeth and a long, stiff tongue. Its body has visible, protruding ribs and he is overall slimy. It also has a dark, uncertain color and its body is rarely seen in full, at least in the movies. The comic books are significantly more detailed.

The Alien is also much more evil and destructive than the other iterations of extraterrestrials that I've described in this chapter, having the ability to overtake a human body. We see proof of this in the infamous scene in the "Alien" movie, where the alien bursts out of the crew member's chest. Thus, here, the extraterrestrial being, takes on the role of a parasite in search of a host, in addition to its independent function and desire for human blood.

Aliens in pop culture today

Nowadays, extraterrestrials are still very much a part of our pop culture. While the craze is nowhere near as heightened as it has been in the past, the question of alien existence has entered the public consciousness. We continue to fantasize based on this assumption or uncertainty of alien existence, in all forms of media. Sci-fi is incredibly popular among people of all ages – girls and boys, men and women. We have conventions, festivals and gatherings and a lot of science fiction stories still feature aliens.

You don't need to look any further than Star Wars, which is enjoying outstanding success with its latest installment, and which is one of the biggest, most popular and most influential movie franchises the world has ever seen. Star Trek was also huge in its day, and it still is. It spawned dozens of TV shows which are meant to replicate this strange and fascinating world of the outer space and its many mysteries. The 90s and 2000s were the height of the interest in outer space, due to the dawn of the new millennium.

Furthermore, we even have shown that are non-fictional, but still, rely on the same alien narrative. Programs like "Ancient Aliens," "UFO Hunters," or the documentary about the secrets of Area 51 are all incredibly impressive and can really make you think. They present information that not everyone may be aware of or even things that can be construed as evidence if you are so inclined to believe. I'm not saying the evidence exists, and I'm not saying that it doesn't – we can't know! But what I am saying is that if you want to hear all the sides of this story and make up your mind, you could give these kinds of shows a watch, considering the fact that they are not fictional.

This just goes to show that until we get some real answers, we will never stop wondering and searching for them. After all, how can we sit around doing nothing, when something this major is potentially happening just a few galaxies away? How would a discovery of intelligent alien life change our lives, our history or the way we perceive the world? We can't know that yet, but we can explore the hypotheticals and the myriad of possibilities, regardless of how far they stretch reality. Sure, you can choose to believe none of it is true, and that is absolutely fine. But oh, what if it is? The fascination with the possibility of alien existence is nowhere near being over.

Chapter 3: The Roswell UFO Incident

In this chapter, you will learn:

- What the Roswell UFO incident is
- What happened and why it sparked such a controversy

What actually happened

Perhaps the most famous UFO-related incident in history is the one that happened at Roswell. Let's rewind for a second – it is the year 1947, and a unique event is taking place in Roswell, New Mexico on July 8th. A strange flying contraption has crashed in the desert, sparking rumors that a so-called "flying saucer" or UFO (Unidentified Flying Object) founds its way on American soil. The reasons that fueled these rumors and hasty conclusions are various, and they include the presence of strange-looking debris, as well as alleged alien corpses.

Although at the time, the incident was promptly explained to be a weather balloon and that put the rumors to rest for a while, the story did not end here. First of all, the explanation given by the military was false, in that the balloon was not a weather one, but it was related to nuclear testing monitoring. The fact that they concealed its true purpose from the public did nothing but fuel the rumor mill regarding what crashed at Roswell on that fateful day in July.

What is assumed to have happened

As time went by, more and more alleged witnesses came forward to give an account of their experience with the Roswell crash. Books were written, and documentaries were made, and although hundreds of people were interviewed, consulted and quoted, only a handful were able to give first-hand or even second-hand accounts of the incident. The details were fuzzy and at times, contradictory, but people described debris, including wood, rubber, and foil, as well as the gray bodies of supposed extraterrestrials.

Also, people had been seeing strange flying saucers in the area weeks before the Roswell incident, which only further convinced the public that the crash had, indeed, been that of an alien spaceship. Coupled with the fact that the military had lied about the flying object, conspiracy theorists reached the conclusion that the government was actively working to hide the fact that America had secret ties with alien beings, that they had contacted Earth, crashed in New Mexico, etc.

The media was in a frenzy over it, as new suppositions were made every day and more people appeared every day, claiming to have seen something or to know someone who had seen something that day or on a different occasion. Of course, none of these accounts were backed by evidence, and Roswell soon became little more than a myth, an urban legend, or, as it was later proven to be, a hoax. It's difficult to say whether or not this was done deliberately, but it is most likely that the incident just took on a life of its own and ran off the rails as time went by.

The next morning, Brazel went to Roswell to sell some of the wool he got from the ranch. He figured that while he was in town, it would probably be wise to report his discovery to Roswell Sheriff George Wilcox, who then passed the message to Major Jesse Marcel of the Roswell Army Air Field. Marcel and an unnamed civilian went with Brazel back to his home where they tried their best to recreate whatever it was that the wreckage came from, but to no avail. They gave up trying to reconstruct the UFO and Maj. Marcel took the debris back to Roswell Air Field with him, and that was the last that Brazel ever saw them again.

The following days, news broke out that the wreckage of an alien UFO was discovered in Roswell, and ever since then the media and alien enthusiasts have started flocking into this once unknown desert town.

Government Cover-up

It was not really clear what it was that Brazel found on his ranch, but it was kind of interesting that the US government suddenly went out and claimed it was the debris of a crashed weather balloon. It was even reported that the army might have harassed Mac Brazel into retracting his first statements and agreeing with the reports that what he saw might have been some kind of experimental weather balloon.

Even Major Marcel said that the debris was unlike anything he ever saw before, and this came from a man who witnessed a multitude of airplanes and rockets in his long career. He was quite certain that they weren't parts of any aircraft he ever saw before.

Project Mogul

In an effort to dispel any doubts from the public, the US government "came clean" and announced that the parts recovered in Roswell, New Mexico came from an experimental, high-altitude surveillance balloon. The information released by the government stated that the balloon's purpose was to spy on the Soviets and warn the United States if ever it detected any nuclear threat.

According to the military, Project Mogul was a top-secret operation whose aim was to strap highly sensitive microphones on high-altitude weather balloons to detect any sound waves that Soviet nuclear bomb tests would have generated.

However, Brigadier General Thomas Dubose, who was present during the press conference that announced Project Mogul, later remarked that "It was a cover story. The whole weather balloon part of it. That was the part of the story we were ordered to give to the public and the news." If that wasn't an admission of guilt, then I don't know what is.

Until now, people are still flocking to Roswell in the hopes that they would catch a glimpse of the alien wreckage, but they will never see it again as it was reportedly whisked off to the infamous Area 51 military base. Was there really an alien spacecraft that crash-landed in Roswell? Since the US government and the military are covering it up to the best of their abilities, odds are we will never find out.

Facts vs. conspiracy theories

But despite the fact that the entire account of the incident has been demonstrated to be false, including the alleged witnessing of gray alien corpses, many ufologists continue to believe that Roswell was real and that the government has yet to come forward with the truth about what actually happened that day. Not only UFO enthusiasts believe it, but also much of the population. A poll conducted in 1997 showed that most of the respondents believed that the balloon that crashed in New Mexico had indeed been an alien spacecraft and that the government was covering it up.

It was the prime time for conspiracy theories and for the growing public opinion that the government was involved in significant and numerous cover-ups meant to mislead the American population and draw their attention away from what was happening. This belief was fueled and supported by a multitude of books written on the subject, each coming up with various theories about what had happened, what was being concealed and the reasons behind the supposed cover-up in 1947. Their sensationalist nature is, of course, far from being trustworthy, but at that point, it was a snowball effect that had gotten out of hand.

More recently, there were two reports carried out by the United States Secretary of the Air Force in 1994 and 1997. Both of them concluded that the remains of the aircraft were from Project Mogul and that any alien corpses that were allegedly seen were simply memories of former dead personnel and injuries conflated with the incident at hand. In other words, no evidence was found of alien bodies or aircraft, dead or alive, in pieces or not. That, however, did not sway the opinion of believers, who deemed the research inconclusive or straight-up false and uninformed.

At the end of the day, no one really knows what exactly happened in Roswell, New Mexico on the 8th of July, 1947. The official statement of the military comes in direct conflict with the stories of the witnesses who are confident of what they saw. And even after a little under 70 years from the incident, it is still not clear who is speaking the truth, who is covering something up and who is involved in a giant hoax that turned into the most well-known UFO claim to date. It is up to each of us to decide what we believe and what we base our belief on.

Chapter 4: The Secrets of Area 51

In this chapter, you will learn:

- What Area 51 is and why it is of interest to ufologists
- What the secrets surrounding Area 51 have created

Area 51 is another ongoing mystery that has sparked conspiracy theories over the years, because of the secretive nature of the establishment and its activities. Located in Southern Nevada, Area 51 is a United States Air Force facility that is part of the Nevada Test and Training Range and the Edwards Air Force Base. The base is top secret, and even the airspace surrounding it is categorized as a restricted area.

This, combined with the fact that no one really knows what purpose the base serves, has led to some interesting suppositions regarding the nature of the facility and what is being hidden from the public as a whole. If we were to look at evidence gathered over the years, the facility is probably developing and testing grounds for weapons systems, as well as experimental aircraft. However, that fact has never been made public, so these are just very well educated guesses.

The reason for all the mystery and conspiracy theories is that people have noticed several unidentified flying objects in the area surrounding the base, which fueled rumors of it serving alien research purposes. The facility was never officially declared secret, but the activity within its walls always has been. All the research is classified as TS/CSI (Top Secret/Sensitive Compartmented Information).

Reality vs. conspiracy – activity at Area 51

The CIA only confirmed the existence of Area 51 as recently as 2013, but the facility has been active for 60 years, having been purchased in 1955. At the time, its purpose was flight testing an aircraft called Lockheed U-2. But conspiracy theories have bloomed over time; here are a few of the most widely spread suppositions regarding the secret activities at Area 51:

- The development and research of means of teleportation and time travel

- The examination, as well as storage, of the materials of the Roswell UFO crash – spacecraft debris and aliens, both dead and alive – plus the development of ships modeled after the alien one

- The planning of the Majestic 12 and one world government

- Creating energy weapons

- The research and creation of weather control technology

- Alien research and meetings

Of course, none of these theories have ever been confirmed, neither officially or unofficially. They remain suppositions or figments of our imagination, or, in the eyes of ufologists, veritable possibilities of the mysterious occurrences at Area 51. Because of the mystery surrounding the facility and the reluctance to reveal the research and activity, conspiracy theorists have no reason to think that their explanations are not real, or at least in the realm of possibility.

You know how it is – when you distrust the government, you are not inclined to believe anything they say, especially if they have something to gain from concealing information from the population. Now, I don't know why the existence of alien life forms would not be revealed – Something about money? Power? State secrets? – But if that doesn't matter information that everyone needs to know about the world we live in, I don't know what is. I mean, I know I would be pretty shocked and angry to find out that all these stories are true and that we have been, indeed, lied to about aliens.

A possible explanation

One interesting aspect is the timeline of UFO sightings. You see, such sightings were suddenly reported with a much higher frequency, apparently confirming the rumored purpose of the Area 51 facility in relation to extraterrestrials or extraterrestrial technology. In reality, here is what happened: at the time (in the mid-20th century), military aircraft flew under 40,000 ft., while civilian ones flew at under 20,000 ft. Once they started testing the Lockheed U-2, which flew at above 60,000 ft., people saw more and more "unidentified flying objects."

Airline pilots, especially, reported sightings in the evening, when the Lockheed U-2 would supposedly reflect the sun setting, and it would make it look like a disc of fire or another similarly strange flying object. Considering the fact that the aim of the base was not revealed, it is understandable that people noticing the U-2 would find the sight uncommon and even unsettling. However, since the facility was being kept a secret, an official explanation could not be given.

In addition, there was also a rumor circulating that there is an underground facility as well, including a transcontinental underground railroad and alien spaceships. These conspiracy theories were and are still supported by several people who claim to have worked at the base, as well as the fact that there are, indeed activities that are carried out underground. Or at least, they used to be. No one really knows what is going on at the base nowadays. Accounts have even reported an alien life form working at the facility; an alien named J-Rod, according to two different men. Of the two, a mechanical engineer said he worked on flying discs based upon alien aircraft, helped by J-Rod. This was recounted in a documentary called "Dreamland." The other man, Dan Burisch, claimed 8 years later, in 2004, to also have worked with the same alien on cloning extraterrestrial viruses. The verisimilitude of these claims has yet to be confirmed.

The existence of J-Rod has never been proven, but multiple accounts are similar and mention this creature's presence. Because of his popularity and the general knowledge of his existence, there have been several theories and suppositions regarding his origin. According to one theory, he is a Grey alien. He ended up here, on Earth, as a result of some sort of exchange program and he was meant to help humans with his extensive knowledge. His use was confirmed by most, if not all the witnesses who claim to have seen him or interacted with him. It is theorized that he was the brains behind several technological advancements we enjoyed in that period, particularly when it comes to the U.S. military and air force.

Another approach is offered by Dan Burisch, one of the men mentioned earlier, who claims to have worked with the alien. According to him, J-Rod was, indeed, a Grey, but there's a twist – he came from the future, and the Grey aliens are evolutionary results of mankind. Supposedly, he was here because the future wasn't very bright and the demise of the Greys was near unless J-Rod was able to undo some of humanity's past mistakes, which would secure its future. While there is no proof of Dan Burisch's recounting, he was assigned to work in S4 in 1994. That certainly lends credibility to his claims.

Something else that Burisch shared was the physical appearance of J-Rod. Allegedly, the Grey was not allowed to wear clothing, so his entire body was visible. His large, egg-like head and huge, black eyes are already present in popular culture, but what is particularly interesting is the description of the alien set of genitals. J-Rod was male, and his genitals were shaped like a disc that would rotate, and which had four protruding areas that would combine with the corresponding four holes in the female genital area. Burisch was able to visualize female Greys with the help of J-Rod, who projected images.

The interesting thing is that Dan Burisch was allegedly abducted at age 9, and he was taken to the spaceship were J-Rod was, so you could definitely say there was a connection there. Burisch was a microbiologist, and he was specially trained to work with J-Rod. Because of his special relationship with him and the occurrences from his childhood, Ron Garner is convinced Burisch communicated with these beings back at home and that he was able to find out secrets that remain otherwise hidden from the general public.

Something very few people know is that these aliens that were present at S4 in Area 51 were toxic, including J-Rod. That is one of the best-kept Black Ops secrets that the aliens couldn't be touched because they were dangerous. That is why J-Rod was kept in an enclosed space, a clean sphere, where he – and everyone outside of it – was completely protected.

S4 – home of the super-secret goings on at Area 51

Area 51 has been discussed and debated to death for decades, but we may have been looking at the problem wrong all along. While it has been more or less confirmed that Area 51 is a military facility dedicated to testing new aircraft models, it is not Area 51 that is of interest here, but a particular part of it, namely S4. This is where the secrets of Area 51 can actually be found; here is where the super-secret stuff is going on, or at least, it used to. That knowledge can be derived from multiple accounts, not least of which is the recollection of Ron Garner in a recent interview, taken before he passed away.

Ron Garner was able to share a lot of information about S4 and what he knew from trusted sources. He was a ufologist for decades before he died, and he had access to information and sources that would blow our collective minds. But something you will notice, from everything I am about to tell you, but also if you go watch an interview yourself, is that all, or nearly all of the sources mentioned were terribly afraid of being discovered. They were threatened. The concept of "men in black" has remained largely a myth over the years, but here is proof that they might, in fact, exist.

Garner tells stories of several people who used to work at Area 51, and more specifically, at S4, who died in highly suspicious circumstances. Whether we're talking about staged suicides, strange disappearances, or weird or unexplained causes of death, all evidence seems to point to the fact that these people were eliminated by the secret government. According to Ron, they've been doing it for over 60 years. Why? Because they knew too much, and possibly shared the information. You will also notice that most of the sources are anonymous, precisely for this reason. People have repeatedly cited being followed or supervised either after having worked in top secret facilities or after having encounters with aliens and telling about them.

A concrete example I can give you, shared by Ron Garner himself, is of a man he knew who used to work at S4 and who swore that a fellow worker told him about a room he wandered into, where he found a strange being with mismatched shoes. The creature supposedly talked to him, complaining that he had to put on that body every day as a cover and that he should get out. The person who told this story also reported being followed by a white van that he thought was the government, or the so-called "men in black," looking to silence him, maybe forever.

But that is far from being the only account of aliens at S4 – Garner also spoke of the International UFO Convention of 1993, that took place in Las Vegas, where he talked to Bill Uhouse. Now, Bill Uhouse turns out to be extremely relevant, because he is an engineer who once worked on a unique project in Los Alamos, at S4, within Area 51. This man claimed that he saw Edward Teller with two creatures from a different start system: a pair of blonde, blue-eyed aliens that are known as "Nordic." Supposedly, they were teaching Teller about the science of their star system. Garner says Edward Teller is on video talking about this.

Ron Garner also touches upon the overall importance that these beings have in our lives and the profound influence they have over major decisions in the world, including wars. They are all influenced by what Garner calls "people not from this star system." But even as different as they are from us, he claims that communication with them is possible and that he himself was married for a decade to a woman who spoke different languages with these beings.

As it was expected, S4 is very, very well guarded, with two separate sets of guards for the inside and outside of the facility. The inside guards are said to be Navy Seals, and allegedly, the changing of the guards is done in complete silence, and perfection, like an automatism. Garner insisted on the strict rules and protocols of the place, and not only when it comes to the guards. Supposedly, you were not allowed to look to your left or right, or step across an individual line – if you did, you got shot on the spot. That's how serious they were.

It went even further – Ron Garner tells stories about how Dan Burisch was weighed every day, when he went in S4 and when he went out. He was stripped down naked and weighed in order to confirm that he had not hidden anything on his body or in his body. That was part of the protocol. Even more interesting is the reason why this was instituted. Before Burisch, John Lear worked there for a short amount of time, and at one point, he brought in a camera and installed it somewhere in the secret facility. He never went back, because he was afraid he wouldn't make it out alive. The camera was eventually discovered, and they set in place the weighing protocol, in order to make sure nothing came in, and nothing went out.

As for what they were working on, to Garner's knowledge, he mentioned Project Looking Glass, which he said was a secret device that allowed the government to see into the past and the future and which also acted as a teleportation device.

There are, undoubtedly, more secrets than we can imagine surrounding Area 51, S4 and extraterrestrial activity. All evidence indicates that we have only begun to scratch the surface of what is a very complex problem that involves a lot of different people, past and present. Unfortunately, Ron Garner passed away shortly after giving his final interview, where I was able to get my information from. Who knows what else he knew and didn't have a chance to share with the world?

Pleiadeans – the better humans

The Nordic aliens Teller was talking about are also called "Pleiadeans," and they are said to be very similar-looking to humans, but originating from different stellar systems which surround the Pleiades stars. They are also supposedly interested in the future of the planet and of mankind. This is a notable difference from most other aliens, which are depicted as either evil or exploiting humans for information and samples. Their intentions were transmitted through certain individuals who claim to have been contacted by the Pleiadeans.

It is unclear where they come from, but it is known that they have some sort of relation with the Lyrians; they might come from their group. According to some sources and theories, Native Americans are descendants of Pleiadeans, and others claim that white people come from Lyrians. Something interesting to note is that they are supposed to be from the third, the fifth, or the ninth dimension, but regardless of where they come from, their goal is to provide aid to mankind, so that they can evolve and get to a higher dimension.

Supposedly, Pleiadeans should look like humans, but better. They are very similar to albinos, in that they have little to no pigmentation in their hair and their skin. They are also said to be similar to Asians, and also Grey aliens. Facial fair is not ordinary, and neither is hair that is not straight, and they are generally fit or even skinny, although female Pleiadeans exhibit some curves.

If we were to go on looks alone, it's tempting to say that Pleiadeans are maybe less likely to be real than others. Why? Precisely because they are so similar to humans. It's simple to imagine that life on a different planet would be like mankind, but better – life is always conceived as better on different planets. This tendency was supported, encouraged and fueled by science fiction, whether it was comics, movies, or TV shows. It made sense for them to look like humans, particularly for TV or film productions, where they used actors and non-elaborate costumes.

Pleiadeans were the change from abduction stories to contact stories, or even channeling stories. That is to say, Nordic aliens don't abduct people (they're trying to help us, remember?), but they are supposedly making efforts to contact us, or even channeling their efforts through human individuals. Of course, this particular trend is a result of its times, with the 1960s being all about love, connection, and togetherness. As we moved on from that, contact turned into channeling, and people started making suppositions of who is or isn't actually a Nordic alien.

You know what I said earlier about being a result of the times? The early-to-mid 20th century was a time of vibrant spirituality, which is where people got the idea that Pleiadeans brought us ear candling, crystal healing, Reiki, Reflexology, Shiatsu, aromatherapy, and even dolphins, for some reason.

They are also said to be related to Lemuria and Atlantis. There have been some far-fetched and controversial statements throughout the years, like the fact that Jesus was a Pleiadean alien, or that Kennedy contacted someone on earth to give us information about Pleiadeans.

Continuing with the idea of the benevolent Pleiadeans, they are allegedly involved in defeating Reptilians, which are evil aliens who are said to be part of the Illuminati. You will remember that several prominent public figures are assumed to be Reptilians or working with the Illuminati.

Chapter 5: Alien Encounters, Abductions, and UFO Sightings

In this chapter, you will learn:

- Why it is important to take notice of people's recollections about aliens

- What aspects of these accounts lends them credibility

Close encounters of the third kind

So, let's say we have zero evidence that aliens have ever landed on Earth or that they exist, at all. We don't know if such proof exists or not, but let's just say it doesn't; work with me, here. We may not have physical evidence, but what about the various accounts of the people who claim to have been abducted by aliens? There are thousands of people who say they have either witnessed extraterrestrial beings landing, that they have met them, that they have been abducted, studied, etc. They can provide detailed descriptions of what they looked like, what they had done to them, what the spacecraft looked like inside and out, etc.

In fact, studies have been done on these people, and they have been put under hypnosis therapy, in order to try to recall as much of their supposed abductions as possible. The results were surprising, as many of them gave very similar accounts. Here are some basic details of these people's stories that I managed to extract:

- Subjects were abducted in their sleep
- Subjects don't remember how they were taken or when
- The memories are fragmented and often don't appear until they are under hypnosis
- Subjects were sexually exploited by aliens, or they had their eggs or sperm collected for breeding/reproductive purposes
- Subjects remember being tested
- Subjects described the experience as being terrifying
- Subjects recall being abducted several times
- Subjects have a very intense emotional response to the abductions
- Subjects described bright lights, levitation, vibrations, and buzzing
- Subjects described the extraterrestrial beings as gray-skinned, with large, oblong heads and big, egg-shaped eyes, and comparatively small bodies

We collectively tend to overlook these recollections or dismiss them as the ramblings of the mentally ill, sleepwalkers, lucid dreamers or people who similarly afflicted or just straight-up are lying. The thing is, these accounts are all described by different people, at different times, in various parts of the world. They are all interviewed individually, so it's not like there's some big conspiracy to prank the whole world into thinking aliens are abducting humans. Something is definitely happening here; we just don't know what. Is it really possible for so many people to experience the same traumatizing, vivid dream?

Even supposing that what they are saying is not true, and they haven't really met aliens, then what happened? How can their experiences be explained to our understanding? If there were any way to do it, they would have been long dismissed by now, but they haven't. People are still coming forward and speaking about their alleged abductions, and we are still fascinated by them every single time. Why? Because we have no other explanation. We either believe that what they say actually happened, or it still remains a mystery, because the phenomenon lacks an explanation.

UFOs and crop circles

Moreover, UFO sightings are reported every day in various parts of the world, not to mention the infamous crop circles that are attributed to aliens. These are occurrences that many people have experienced and, more importantly, that cannot be easily explained away in any logical manner. While some of those UFO sightings are definitely people mistaking other aircraft for alien spaceships, a lot of them remain complete mysteries and go unexplained. It is not a coincidence that so many people, in so many places, seem to witness these unidentified flying objects. It must mean something.

And coming back to crop circles... what is that all about? I mean, there is no possible explanation for them. No one ever sees anyone creating them in the dead of night – and they always appear overnight. The strongest arguments supporting the theory that crop circles are created by aliens are, a) they appear suddenly, overnight, although making a crop circle is laborious work that would take forever, b) they are always perfect and symmetrical, and c) they are not shapes that mean anything in our terrestrial world, but they do appear to be encoded messages. We have not yet been able to crack the code, but the shapes are definitely not chosen at random.

So, what are they, then? A very elaborate prank? That would be quite a stunt to pull off, especially considering the fact that these crop circles have appeared all over the world, not just in one place. That would mean that multiple people, from multiple cultures, had the same kooky idea, ways to create them and the skill it requires to execute them flawlessly. In addition, these shapes tend to appear in the middle of nowhere or on some godforsaken farm. Personally, I don't think Farmer Bob is much of an expert troll and would be able to pull off a hoax of this magnitude. Do you?

Chapter 6: Testimonies and Stories

In this chapter, you will learn:

- About abductees and collective testimonies
- Details about some of the most exciting and well-known abduction stories

When lies are lies, and the truth is still lies

So far, the only "evidence" (if it can be called that) we have that indicates the existence of extraterrestrials is based on witness testimonies, claims, and stories. More specifically, I'm talking about stories of alien abduction. I'm sure you've heard them before or at least heard about them. There are thousands of people who have made such claims over the years, some more successful than others. While a few of them were discredited or proven to be lying for attention, fame, money or whatever else they were trying to obtain, other cases are less cut and dry. It's easy to dismiss these stories as being made up, but it's not nearly as clear as you think it would be.

There is a compelling and fascinating psychological component at work here. For example, some of these people were proven to be lying by making them take the polygraph test, also known as a lie detector. Now, this machine bases its results on the changes occurring in your body. It does not automatically detect lies, but merely deceptive behavior. That's why they ask naturally honest questions in the beginning, in order to establish a baseline. When you're telling the truth, your brain is at rest, because the truth does not require stretching the facts. When it comes to lying, however, the brain starts working in overdrive, which causes the physical reactions, such as sweating, blushing, increased heart rate, blinking, etc.

But – and there is a critical "but" here – what happens when a person genuinely believes the lie they are telling? You got it; the polygraph does not detect any "lies" because your brain does not realize you are telling them. Thus, separating a person who is telling the truth from one who is simply delusional can be extremely difficult, especially given the fact that these events involving aliens don't tend to have a lot of witnesses and cannot be proven to have happened. So, unless the person has an alibi provided by another individual who was with them at all times and can demonstrate that they are lying, we have no other choice than to believe them – or not – based on personal biases or gut feelings.

See for yourself

So, then what now? Do we believe everyone? Do we dismiss everyone? Do we maintain a healthy dose of skepticism? I can't decide that for you because that's something only you know. Each person is allowed to decide for themselves whether they believe or not. I'm not going to claim to know either way (because I don't), so the easiest and most logical thing to do is to introduce you to some of these testimonies. The thing that convinces most people is the fact that these stories tend a) to be very detailed and very descriptive and b) to all have similar details. Of course, this can either mean that different people have experienced different things, or it can mean that some people are copying others or are subconsciously influenced by the details of other people's stories.

One thing that is fascinating about these types of recollections is that a lot of these persons claim to have been abducted or reached by alien forces multiple times over the course of their lives, sometimes even together with their families. In more morbid cases, some of them end up dying from unnatural and mysterious causes, including unknown viruses.

So, instead of blabbing about it forever, I'm going to allow you to make up your own minds, based on the facts or fiction that these people have presented over the years.

- **Barney and Betty Hill, 1961** – The abduction story of Barney and Betty Hill is, perhaps, one of the most famous among the UFO community. It happened way back in 1961, and it's one of those eerie happenings that no one can explain. Actually, an explanation does exist, but no one can *prove* it. Herein lies the rub. You see, Barney and Betty were a married couple driving home from a brief vacation in Canada. They were in their car, several hours from home when they saw something strange up in the sky. Barney tried to convince himself it was a weird-looking plane (disc-shaped, flying erratically); Betty thought otherwise.

   While "aliens" never went through their heads at the time, Betty did think that it seemed more like a strange flying object and nothing like a plane. They saw it intermittently through the trees, and Barney got to take a look at it close enough through his binoculars. He noticed that the aircraft was, indeed circular, surrounded by windows and the passengers aboard it could be seen clearly. They did not look human. Alarmed, he ran back to the car where he had left his wife and sped home.

   The flying object could not be seen anymore, but they did hear a beep. Upon hearing the second beep, the couple suddenly noticed that a full two hours had passed. Not only that, but they were several miles ahead of the road. The night passed without any more incidents, but this would not be the end of the story for the two spouses. Betty started having terrible nightmares about being taken to the aircraft against their will and examined by the inhabitants of the ship.

They were described as humanoid, with dark hair and eyes, but gray skin and blue lips.

Her dreams included several details that can maybe be considered irrelevant, since they were dreams, and she could have just imagined them all. What she couldn't have imagined, however, were the very real material signs of some sort of unexpected encounter, as well as the two missing hours. Several of their belongings were inexplicably damaged or broken (Barney's binoculars, his shoes, Betty's dress) and there was some strange, powdery residue on Betty's skirt. This residue was examined by as many as five different laboratories, over time. Barney was later put under hypnosis and recalled the same encounter Betty dreamed about. Conclusions from his hypnotist indicated that he unknowingly took inspiration from his wife's stories during his regression therapy, although he disagreed.

- **Michael and Janet, Buff Ledge, 1968** – Buff Ledge was a girls' camp and Michael and Janet both worked there. One evening, the two were sitting around the lake, looking at the sunset, when they saw a dazzling light in the sky. At first, it seemed as though Venus itself was falling down from the sky, but soon the light created three new lights that started moving as if they were controlled by something or someone. They witnessed how two of them disappeared, as well as the big, bright one, leaving one that was closer than ever.

It was now apparent that this was an object; a saucer-like aircraft, with a glass dome on top and some small creatures in it, that could be seen staring at the two teenagers. Michael recalls that they were bald, with big heads and long necks, as well as large eyes. He seemed to be able to mentally communicate with them, as the craft shone a very bright beam on them. This prompted him to become very scared about the possibility of being kidnapped, so he pulled Janet back and started yelling that he didn't want to go.

The next thing they both remember, however, is staring at this object from afar, only the sky was now dark. The two teenagers had no idea how much time had passed or what happened. Janet also seemed to be in a trance. They watched the aircraft fly away into the night and didn't bring up the events of the evening for the next few weeks. They were not sure what they had seen.

Several years later, however, Michael contacted the Center for UFO Studies; he'd been having dreams of being abducted. So, he was put under regressive hypnosis, in order to bring back these memories, if they existed. Michael remembered his experience of being lifted from the ground by that beam and transported into the craft, Janet being examined on a table and other details that match the accounts of other supposed abductees. When put under the same therapy, Janet confirmed Michael's report. Upon further investigation, other campers had noticed the strange lights and objects too, that summer, so the story is confirmed.

- **The Doraty Family, 1973** – In May 1973, Judy Doraty, Cindy Doraty (her daughter), as well as Judy's sister in law and mother were returning from Bingo in Houston, Texas. When they started the journey home, they didn't know they would have the strangest encounter of their lives. They were all going to Texas City, to Judy's house, but they first took a detour to Alto Loma to get Judy's sister and her husband at home.

  They made the stop successfully and the four remaining continued on their way when they suddenly noticed a light hovering over them. It was strange, so they stopped to look at it for a while before it disappeared. They went on back home to Texas City. At the time, it seemed like there was nothing more to it, but they would be wrong.

Judy soon started having anxiety, as well as severe headaches. She went through multiple doctors who dismissed her symptoms before she got to work with Dr. Leo Sprinkle, who was not only a hypnotist but also a ufologist. He would be able to help her realize what was going on. The doctor made a recommendation for hypnosis but didn't tell Judy what he suspected right away – that this was the aftermath of an alien abduction.

Sure enough, under the influence of hypnosis, Judy was able to remember that she had encountered a UFO of some kind, as well as its inhabitants – two small entities that reportedly sliced up a cow. She could also remember feeling like she was in two places at the same time: inside the aircraft and right beside her car. Her recollections would be later used in a documentary called "Strange Harvests."

Judy described the aliens as being gray, around four feet tall, with big heads shaped like an egg. Judy also recounted familiar imagery in abduction stories – her daughter lying on an operating table and the strange little creatures taking samples. Years later, Cindy would undergo hypnosis herself and tell the same story as her mother.

As with all such cases, not all the abductees remember the event. Judy reported 16 witnesses, but no one else seems to remember, except for her and her daughter. The Texas Airforce base was of no help, either, as they didn't acknowledge anything appearing on the radar on that May night, in 1973.

Judy was reluctant to give details about her experience because of the way her story was received by those around her. People, including her family, ridiculed her and her alleged encounter, and she was shy about telling others, yet. But she did remember vivid, important details, like a small gray alien who gave her a formula, the calf that got mutilated, the way she was transported into the craft, the impossibly bright light – these were all things that would stick with her for a long time to come.

Much later, Judy Doraty learned why she was not given much interest or a second look – the government warned her indirectly not to say anything about her abduction, and especially about the formula she received.

- **Alan Godfrey, 1980** – Across the Pond, Alan Godfrey was in his police car, driving along the road, when he saw a very bright light. This was later confirmed and called in by two other sources, so at least this part of the story checks out. As he drove closer and closer, it became apparent that this was an object, which he took to drawing on the spot. It fit the description and the drawings of most of the abductees: a large, saucer-like aircraft with a dome on top and windows all around. At this point, the car was stopped, but then he was suddenly driving again, past the place where the object had landed. He had missed some time that he could not account for.

Returning to the spot where the aircraft had been, he noticed that the ground was wet, even though it wasn't raining that night. It was later established that the missing time was no longer than 15 minutes. Alan did not report his experience right away, because of his position and because he didn't want to be made fun of for this strange experience that he could not identify. However, after finding out that others had similar accounts, he decided to come forward.

Like many others in his position, he was put under regression hypnosis, and he was able to remember being brought aboard the craft and interacting with the creatures that inhabited it. They fit the image of the "traditional" Grays, although Godfrey claimed they also had beards and that there were several smaller men around, looking like robots. He recalled a man named Yosef, who argued that they would have other encounters. Unlike many other accounts – particularly American ones – he claimed he was not studied.

The abductee admitted that he was unsure if this recollection was real, imagined or a dream sequence, but he was certain of the reality of his experience. However, he sadly suffered undue consequences due to his experience, including having to resign from the police force, even though psychological tests indicated that he was perfectly capable of doing his job and mentally sound.

- **Hudson Valley, 1987** – Connecticut, New Jersey, and New York witnessed a growing number of reports of UFO sightings, especially in the 1980s. It might even be one of the highest in the world. Of all these sightings, a fair share were actually abductions. These accounts will remain anonymous as the names have been changed in order to protect the identity of the witnesses.

Gail was lying in bed on a night in June 1987 when she started feeling like she was being watched. A voice said that they'd come for her, but not hurt her. That was understandably distressing, but not as much as the fact that now her body was paralyzed, and her eyes were the only ones she could move. Three silhouettes appeared before her, one behind the other, dressed in some kind of tight suits. She described them as five feet tall, with long arms, but she could not distinguish their features.

They tried passing into the room but were stopped by a shield that was invisible. One of the figures pressed his hands on it, then took out a multi-colored rod that he passed across the door. The shield had vanished, and he entered the room. Gail could now distinguish their features as cat eyes and big heads. They couldn't be heard talking, but her head buzzed when the three communicated. They surrounded her bed, put their hands under her and lifted her. Soon, one of them put a white tube up her nose, and she lost consciousness.

When she woke up, it was morning; her nose was bleeding, and her head hurt. The mirror showed her that her nose had swollen, and her arms, legs, and neck had a rash.

Her daughter returned later from her trip and recounted her own story of being followed by a triangular aircraft on the very same night. The girl had been with her father, and they missed half an hour that cannot be accounted for. Sometime after, Gail reported the same occurrence, in the same way, in the same circumstances.

- **Kelly Cahill, 1993** – An incident remarkably similar to the others recounted here happened down under, as well, in Australia, as recently as 1993. Kelly Cahill and her family (her husband and their three children) were in the car, on their way home. Suddenly, some colorful lights appeared, coming from an aircraft that had a rounded shape and windows all around. Kelly thought she could even see the people inside.

At this point, the family was already frightened, but they had no other recourse than to continue driving, hoping to get to safety. But they were soon met by another bright light, a blinding one that almost made night appear as if it were day. Resolved to keep driving, they did not stop but instead were soon strangely calm, and the bright light had disappeared.

Realizing that she was missing some crucial pieces of information, she assumed she had blacked out, but her husband could not confirm that for her; he could not remember, either. The family continued their ride home without any other strange encounters, but upon arriving back and changing for bed, Kelly discovered that she had a mark on her navel that hadn't been there before – a triangle.

The next few weeks did not get easier, as the woman started suffering from stomach pains and uterine infections and made repeated trips to the hospital. Around this time, she also started remembering what has happened during those hours that were missing from their collective memory. She was able to describe the UFO and its location and remembered them stopping the car and leaving it to walk towards the light.

The creatures she encountered were described as lacking a soul and having a black-ish color. They were also tall and had massive eyes with a red glow. It is important to note a few things here. First, Kelly was able to remember all of this without any help from anyone. These were her own memories. Another thing is that there was a second car stopped on the side of the road that Kelly could remember. The kicker? The people in the other car were 100% real, and they told the exact same story as Kelly.

The field was crawling with these beings that Kelly felt were evil. Both she and the other family told stories of how they were abducted, controlled and had procedures performed on them against their will. Among them, Kelly recalls being stripped down and one of the aliens doing something to her navel; that explains the mark she discovered later that night. The next thing she recounts is going unconscious and then waking up back in the car, driving home. Her story was never disproven, nor was it accepted as indisputably true.

- **Philip Schneider's encounter testimonies, 1979** – The problem with this story is that it's told by one man, with little evidence provided, instead of being a reported and registered incident in the official channels. However, the information and the allegations expressed by Phil Schneider are some of the craziest, most incredible stories you can find in the UFO community, whether you choose to believe him or not, and this is why I have to make a mention of him. Schneider was a geologist and engineer who claimed to have worked for the US government on various black budget projects, particularly, on building secretive, underground military installations and bases. According to him, there are over 130 underground bases throughout the United States. He claimed to have been tasked mostly with the use of explosive ordinance used during the underground construction processes.

Schneider is one of the people who has popularized a number of theories I mentioned earlier, especially concerning Area 51, where he claimed to have worked, among other places. Some of those stories include the presence of and contact with aliens at Area 51, the alleged intercontinental underground railway systems, the alien J-Rod, etc. He also said that there are nine underground military installations at Area 51.

His most well-known encounter story allegedly happened in 1979, when he was assigned to work on the construction of more underground facilities at the so-called Dulce Base, in New Mexico. According to proponents of this theory, Dulce is a military base jointly operated by humans and aliens and is home to a large bioengineering laboratory. Now, apart from the government's knowledge and interaction with alien species, including the grays and ten other kinds, there is an even more incredible aspect of his story. Allegedly, there is an actual underground war going on there between certain elements of the US military and a number of alien species, who have been stationed underground for over four hundred years. Schneider claimed that there was a significant engagement at Dulce in August 1979, which left sixty-six agents and employees of the government dead and started this war.

As the story goes, on a particular day, Schneider went down underground on an elevator and encountered three gray aliens, whom he described as around seven feet tall and emitting a pungent, foul smell. He said he reached for his issue pistol and managed to take down two of the creatures, while the third one launched some sort of beam at him. According to Schneider, the impact of this beam is what cost him the two fingers missing from his left hand, and inflicted a near-fatal wound on his lower body. Schneider's grief is that the US government was well aware of the existence of these eleven species of alien life forms underground, but did nothing to inform or warn him and the other personnel working on these underground projects. Of these alien races, two are friendly and cooperative, he says.

One of these friendly species is the alleged Nordic aliens, who originally come from the Pleiades star cluster and are very humanoid in appearance as well as helpful and considerate. On at least one occasion, Schneider even named one of these extraterrestrials, Val Valiant Thor, who has worked for the US government and military for most of the 20th century, with a lifespan of over four hundred years. Schneider describes him as a human-like person of incredible intelligence and a few different physical properties, mostly concerning his biology. He even shows a photo in one of his lectures, which he alleges shows the humanoid alien sitting at some sort of a conference with many scientists who worked on the development of nuclear weapons at the time.

All in all, Philip Schneider's account revolves around a deep, longstanding interaction between many of the world's governments and a variety of different aliens. Allegedly, a lot of the military technology that has been developed over the decades, such as stealth aircraft, directly utilizes technology recovered from aliens. Furthermore, he alleges that it's possible that some of the most dangerous diseases that we are still combating may have been brought over by some of these aliens, as a lot of them carry germs and bacteria that are very dangerous to humans, and vice-versa.

It's purported by some that Philip Schneider was the target of numerous assassination attempts during his years of whistleblowing and holding public lectures and conferences. Finally, he was found dead inside his apartment in 1996, after dying under what many agree were suspicious circumstances. His death had been ruled out as a suicide, but it is strange indeed that he was found with a simple catheter tied around his neck, which suggested strangling.

As far as his allegations against the government are concerned, his numerous lectures have been documented and can easily be found on the internet. As always, it should only be up to you to analyze the information and evidence he provided and make up your own mind as to their validity.

- **Robert Taylor, 1979** – This is one rather convincing story that was widely reported on. Robert was a forest worker in Scotland at the time, perceived by those who knew him as an earnest, well-mannered man who took his work seriously. In other words, he was not considered to be the kind of person to go around making up wild stories, least of all for publicity.

On the morning of November 9, which he probably expected to be just another uneventful day in the forest, Robert had what appears as an encounter with aliens by all indicators. While he was strolling through the woods with his dog, he suddenly came face to face with a UFO. The object or craft emitted no sound and showed no motion whatsoever. Instead, it was merely hovering just above the ground in a field, appearing to be parked. Needless to say, the man was in awe, but he gave a fairly detailed description of the UFO later on.

The object was engaging in what seemed to Robert as some sort of a camouflage countermeasure, almost as if it was trying to morph and blend itself into the background. The UFO was round in shape, and it had a ring roughly around its middle. According to Robert's impression, it was some twelve feet in height and twenty feet wide. Its outer shell was not smooth but had some kind of texture, and apart from a few lit up areas, the craft was gray.

While the UFO itself made no maneuvers in reaction to Robert's presence, two round, spiked objects suddenly came right at him from the main craft. These were smaller in size but still resembled the large UFO. The spheres made noise as they rushed towards him, before somehow taking him by his pants and beginning to drag him towards the mysterious object. Robert also reported that he could detect a foul smell just before he passed out.

The next thing he recalled was waking up to his dog frantically barking, visibly disturbed by whatever happened. The mysterious objects were nowhere to be seen. Robert reported that his whole body felt so weak that he had to crawl at first before he could get up on his feet again and that his vocal cords had been all but disabled in the immediate aftermath of the incident. His loss of voice made him unable to report what had just transpired from his radio in the truck. To make matters more hopeless, his truck got bogged down as he was trying to make his way back to the HQ, forcing him to go back to his house on foot.

When he finally made it home within about an hour, his wife said that he looked a muddy and torn up mess. Although he still felt physically sick, his voice began to come back, and he was able to get in touch with his supervisor, after refusing his wife's advice to report the incident to the police. Reportedly, he elected not to call the police because he felt they wouldn't take him seriously, which, in my opinion, works towards his credibility.

His boss got in touch with a doctor and went over to Robert's house right away. After hearing Robert's incredible story, he went and tried to find the location of the incident on his own, while Robert waited for the doctor. The doctor determined that he suffered no head injuries and that all of his vitals were within their bounds. Meanwhile, Robert's boss was unable to locate the site on his own.

Soon after that, Robert took his supervisor back to the location of the encounter, where they found strange, unfamiliar imprints on the ground. Since both of the men were now convinced, they decided to call the police. Subsequent police inquiries produced two interesting results. Firstly, they were able to confirm that no aircraft, whether commercial or military, were recorded flying in that area that morning. Secondly, even the police were unable to identify the marks that were found at the scene of the supposed encounter.

The marks left by the unknown objects included two lines, which resembled ladders and ran parallel for a couple of meters, with forty holes along the tracks themselves! This is interesting because it may corroborate Robert's story even further, as the objects that he claimed came at him were spherical, rolling on their spikes as they attacked.

Either way, the fact that these strange marks were found there definitely proves that something was on that field. Unfortunately, that's as good as the evidence gets in this case, and we are left only with the aftermath and Robert's account, which he gave again in at least one recorded interview. It was also estimated later on that Robert was passed out for around twenty minutes during the incident, which would also make up his time being abducted, if true.

- **George Gatay, 1954** – This particular incident reportedly occurred in Nouatre, which is a town in western France. Gatay was a respectable member of his community and a veteran of World War II, who had been working at a local construction site at the time. His shift on September 30, 1954, was to be unlike any other until and after then. Gatay was in charge of a crew of eight men who were all with him that day, going about their work duties as per usual.

  In the afternoon hours of that day, he told, Gatay was suddenly overcome with an unexpected and strange drowsiness that came out of nowhere. Just as it came over him, he simply began to walk away from the others, without a clear idea of where he was going or why; almost as if he was just drawn away by something. After only a short while of walking by himself, Gatay saw a peculiar individual standing on an elevated area not very far in front of him. The individual, or creature, was described as having a stained glass helmet on his head, wearing a strange, gray suit that looked like some sort of a utility jumpsuit coverall with an electronic device or display on the chest area, as well as a pair of boots. This perceived spaceman was also wielding a strange-looking rod in his hand, apparently a sort of weapon according to Gatay.

Hovering motionlessly behind the mysterious figure, just a couple of feet above ground, was an unidentified object that had a dome shape to it. On top of the central dome itself was a second, smaller one, described as also having some sort of spikes on top of it, the likes of antennas or some other device. Gatay stood in awe of what was before him. Finding himself completely stilled by sight, he continued to observe the apparent alien for a short while. He later explained that although the idea of running away had crossed his mind, he felt paralyzed and unable to make a move.

Soon after that, Gatay explained, this strange figure simply disappeared, without moving in any way to physically leave the scene. Rather, the alien just vanished from sight as if instantly erased from existence. Right after that, a loud noise in the form of a whistle resonated through the area, snuffing out all the other sounds in the construction site. The dome-shaped UFO then began to rise upwards, yanking itself towards the sky in a string of sudden, sharp motions. After it had gained some altitude, the craft also just disappeared from sight, leaving behind what Gatay described as a cloud of blue mist.

While his puzzling paralysis during the encounter could simply be attributed to fear or shock, that would still fail to explain the sudden feeling of fatigue before he even saw anything in the first place. Particularly interesting is the fact that the rest of the crew later also reported that they had a similar feeling around the same time. Either way, after the UFO made its exit,

Gatay could move again, as if he was freed from some kind of shackle. He immediately ran back to his colleagues, shouting, asking if they had seen anything strange at all. Indeed, one of the men confirmed seeing what he described as a flying saucer, while another even spoke of the mystery man that Gatay ran into. He said the man looked like he was dressed for diving underwater. The rest of Gatay's crew all agreed that the strange incident had indeed just transpired. The men from the construction crew also said that they had been highly skeptical of the whole UFO phenomenon prior to this event.

For roughly a week following this encounter of the third kind, Gatay said he suffered a range of physical symptoms such as intense headaches, poor appetite, and even insomnia.

There is a variety of factors to consider when it comes to judging the credibility of this particular incident. Firstly, much like in the case of Robert Taylor, Gatay was a respectable man who didn't have any apparent cause to make up stories. He was a man of good work etiquette and mature disposition, who served his country in World War II and was even wounded in action. More importantly, of course, his whole crew corroborated his story, though some of the men still didn't believe it was an alien craft per se. Instead, they figured it could have been an experimental military aircraft. Be that as it may, what matters is that they all reported the sighting was accurate. Gatay's and his crew's encounter remains to this day one of the unexplained ones, still waiting to be debunked by anybody. Therefore, it remains a matter of personal choice whether you want to believe it or not.

Finally, one last interesting fact to note is the bigger picture of that particular time. Starting on September 12 of 1954, there was a recorded wave of UFO sightings throughout western and southern Europe, which persisted all the way into late November of the same year. Reports kept coming out of a few countries in this region, most of which were, in fact, from France. So, Gatay's sighting is just one in a series of incidents that occurred at that time. Was this great wave of sightings due to an uptick in military experimentation with classified technology? Was it, perhaps, just a mass panic induced by the Cold War scare of that era? Or were those sightings legitimate encounters with extraterrestrial visitors? As is always the case, we're left with testimonies, very little to no physical evidence and a lot of room for speculation on those cases that are yet to be explained away by science.

- **The Gundiah property, 2001** – October 4th and October 5^{th,} 2001 hold a special significance to Keith Rylance, Amy, and Petra Heller, business partner of the two. They are all on the Gundiah property, with Keith and Petra having gone to sleep in their respective bedrooms, while Amy, Keith's wife, remained in the lounge to watch TV and fell asleep on the couch. There was a storm that night.

  At around 11 pm, approximately 1 hour – 1 hour and a half after the three had fallen asleep, Petra was awoken and found the lounge full of a very bright rectangular light that was coming in through the window. Petra saw Amy being lifted and carried out within the beam, while still asleep. She also saw the objects that had been left on the coffee table and had come to notice the flying disc that was projecting the light, before fainting.

  She soon regained consciousness and screamed, which woke Keith up. He, too, says he saw the objects that had been on the coffee table, only they were in front of the window, on the floor. The window was torn, Amy was nowhere to be found, and Petra was crying, so he went out to look for his wife. Keith didn't believe Petra's hysterical explanations, so he called the police.

It took 1 hour and a half for the police to arrive at a scene that seemed like it might have been a murder, but which was claimed to be an alien abduction. But that was hard to believe. Three officers were present at the scene, examining the torn window, as well as some flower bushes that had been affected. Meanwhile, Keith received a call from a woman in Mackay, which is 800 kilometers away, claiming to have found Amy, who was fine and had been examined by a doctor.

Amy later gave a statement to the Mackay police, saying she remembered being on the couch watching TV and then found herself on a bench in a room that was heavily lighted. She said she called out and was answered by a male voice which assured her everything was fine, before appearing in front of her as a 6-foot tall man. He wore a bodysuit and a black mask. He told her they were leaving her not far off from where they took her. After that, she fell asleep.

The next thing she knows is waking up somewhere she didn't recognize. While Amy said this hadn't happened before, she had a UFO sighting as a child. Upon her husband's arrival, he noted marks on her body: on her heels, and on her inner thigh, in a triangular shape. Perhaps the most interesting and unusual thing is that her hair had grown – both on her head and on her body, suggesting that maybe time had passed differently for her.

The case took a weird turn when Keith Rylance started to give signs that he wanted to be in control of the way the investigation was being carried out and the way the story would get handled in the media. He wanted to get the story to the press, although the investigators were against it.

The investigators traveled to the property in the absence of the witnesses and found some things that advance the general strangeness even further. There was a dog there, and he seemed to have been prone to jumping on the window, including the one that had been damaged when Amy was supposedly lifted. Furthermore, the plant that had supported damage was apparently commonly damaged by sunlight, according to the gardener.

After this, neither Keith nor Amy responded to calls, and they were not willing to keep talking about the case and the experience. A possibility hinted at by Keith is that "men in black" came and threatened them, which scared them into silence.

Chapter 7: Alien Civilizations & The New World Order and the Majestic 12

In this chapter, you will learn:

- What the New World Order is and what it seeks to accomplish

- What alien civilizations have to do with a possible invasion

Are alien civilizations good or bad?

One question that appears over and over, when it comes to extraterrestrial life, is how advanced they are, exactly and how old their civilization is. I mean, compared to the life of our own planet, which is young, we are mere babies. Now think of old planets in the galaxy and how old possible alien civilizations could be. They could be millions of years in the making; we can't even comprehend the level of advancement that they might have. In fact, some believe that ancient aliens visited planet Earth and that they contributed to our own advancement, but that's a theory we will be discussing in the next chapter.

Conspiracy theorists believe that while there are various intelligent and advanced alien civilizations in the universe, some of them are benevolent while others are not. I don't know if "evil" is the right word to use here because this is not a movie and these are not bad guys. But it has been supposed that the stories of abductions we hear are not only true but that they have been facilitated by the U.S. government, who exchanged civilians for technology. This would tie in with the Area 51 theories on alien technology, working with J-Rod and developing top secret aircraft.

It seems like people never think that aliens visit without our knowledge or permission; the popular theory is that they are either invited or permitted by our leaders to come, study us, use us for research, etc. This would also act as a possible explanation for the crop circles we talked about earlier, in a previous chapter, not to mention the fact that it would account for all the UFO sightings no one ever looks into, as well as the infamous Roswell incident that was supposedly covered up. There are many variables to this issue, and perhaps this theory doesn't get all of them right, but at least for a few of them, the proverbial shoe definitely fits.

The New World Order

Perhaps most importantly, this theory of alien civilizations – particularly the malevolent ones – fits right in with the New World Order (NWO) conspiracy theory. You see, some people believe that there is a world government in the making, a totalitarian one. Supposedly, the secret elite is working to overthrow every government in the world and create a new world government that will rule the entire world and will have absolute power. Consequently, all kinds of activity in fields like finance or politics are believed to be intentionally and carefully planned by the powers to be. Everything is a possible move on the part of the elite to further their plan. You may have heard of people talking about Masons, the Illuminati or The Elders of Zion – these are all different facets of the same NWO theory. Of course, like most conspiracy theories, this one may have gone a little off the rails, and the Illuminati connection, especially, is openly ridiculed by most people.

Now, it's easy to dismiss such a seemingly ridiculous claim – really evil people who are trying to take over the world? It sounds like a cartoon villain – but it is not outside the realm of possibility that behind the scenes, there are discussions and plans taking place. We probably can't even imagine what the wealthy and powerful are actually capable of and what they influence without us even knowing. But until there is some kind of mass uncovering of the truth, all we can do is speculate.

Ron Garner, ufologist, had some secrets to spill regarding the New World Order and Majestic 12. You see, he confirmed that the New World Order is comprised of extraterrestrials, but there is a catch – according to him, an extraterrestrial is not the same as alien. The latter is an entirely different being from humans, a new organism that was developed separately. An extraterrestrial, on the other hand, is a human from the future. That may be the explanation behind the alleged secret plan to take over the world, after all; they're not aliens – why would aliens want our planet and our society? – but humans, only from the future.

What would such a force win by overthrowing world governments and creating a universal one? Well, absolute power. It's certainly a very attractive deal to many, but is this really possible in real life? It's worth noting that the two primary supporting groups furthering this theory are both American: Christian fundamentalists, along with anti-government militants, both concerned with the end of times. Thoroughly convinced in the Apocalypse and the impending second coming of Jesus, these people believe that the emergence and installment into the power of the New World Order are the final piece of the puzzle before the coming of the Antichrist. You may or may not believe in such things, but this is not all.

The Reptilian or Gray invasion

"But what does this have to do with aliens?" you might rightfully ask. Well, they are connected in a number of different ways, and this is where theories differ. Remember when I talked about the Lizard People earlier in the book? The Reptilian aliens? Well, here is where they fit in. Some of the believers in the NWO claim that the real plan is for aliens to come into power on Earth. Basically, an alien invasion is supposedly being orchestrated as we speak. Many of them are convinced that some of the most powerful figures on the planet are, in fact, aliens - the President of the United States, Barack Obama, Queen Elizabeth of England, or Pope Francis are just a few of the most high-profile examples.

Some theorists often tie the existence of Reptilians to the supposed Illuminati secret society, so it's not uncommon for certain people to argue that other public figures are also part of this cabal. A number of such individuals are not all that public, though, but are very powerful nonetheless. These are usually said to be the wealthiest bloodlines in the world, such as the Rockefellers and Rothschilds, who use their funds, influence, and banking connections to alter the course of global politics either for personal gain or a higher goal unknown to us.

Since the theories revolving around the Illuminati are very prevalent nowadays, to the point of treading into the ridiculous, it's not unheard of for theorists to proclaim that many celebrities are also involved with the secret society. It's difficult to gather exactly how much truth there is to these claims if any and even more so to determine how much these theories relate to the so-called Reptilians infiltrators. This is mainly because the allegations are so wildly spread by the public and are often contributed to by pranksters, hoaxers, and internet trolls, coupled with a lack of any substantial evidence.

Whether they are Reptilians or Grays depends on the group of believers. Does this mean that the Antichrist is a Gray or a Reptilian? It's not clear.

What is clear is that people are scared of these shape-shifting extraterrestrials, who they think are being helped by the Majestic 12. What is the Majestic 12? The shadow government who is doing all the "dirty work," so to speak, so that our alien overlords can come and claim their new planet. The Majestic 12 is also supposedly the one who green-lights alien abductions, makes evidence disappear and discredits the accounts of people who were kidnapped and tested.

The Majestic 12 is used to explain the mysteries of Area 51 and the alien that was said to be working there, J-Rod. According to the conspiracy theory, the shadow government is allowing the abductions and shift in power in exchange for information and technology. That would fit right in with the claims that J-Rod was the one feeding information and working on model spaceships. It would also lend credibility to the Roswell incident.

The Majestic 12 – the reveal of the current members

For decades, the Majestic 12 was no more than a glimmer in the eye of conspiracy theorists. The suppositions existed, but no one could say anything for sure because no evidence was ever unearthed. In fact, no one ever even came out to claim that they could confirm the Majestic 12 is real or not. And while that may be because it's just a figment of our collective imagination, it might also be because the government is, indeed, actively trying to suppress those who know "too much."

Well, after years of silence on the topic, with no more than vague speculations to go on, there is a person who was able to break it, and that is Ron Garner. He shed light on a number of different things when it comes to ufology and aliens. After a prolific career as a ufologist, you expect the man to have seen some things and have some interesting stories. And he had; in fact, he recounted them in an exclusive interview practically on his deathbed, as he sadly passed away right after he finished sharing this valuable information.

The infamous interview is lengthy and informative, and it touches upon many different aspects, but perhaps most interestingly, upon the Majestic 12. Not only the organization itself but its current members and insight into its objectives. You see, Garner even introduces new information: Europe has its own version of the Majestic 12, called The Committee of the Majority. We also learn that Europe is engaged in a lot more research on this matter than the United States, and Ron is of the opinion that it's because the secret government doesn't have as much control there as it does in America.

But more importantly, Ron Garner was able to provide us with a list of names – that's right, he gave a list of 12 names that belong to the people he claims are currently members of the Majestic 12. The list is interesting, to say the least, and it may provide insight into some of the happenings around the world, especially in the United States. If you look at the list provided below, you will notice that each and every one of these names belongs to an influential person who may have influenced history, albeit from the shadows. These 12 people are currently believed to live both in the public eye and hidden from it, quietly pulling the strings, not only on the issue of aliens, UFOs, and public knowledge about them but on many other things that we cannot even begin to comprehend.

The following is a list of names of the Twelve alleged members, along with their positions and titles, as claimed by Ron Garner in his interview:

1) Former vice admiral of the US Navy John Michael McConnell, who served as the Director of National Intelligence within George W. Bush's administration.

McConnell was also the director of the NSA in the 1990s, during his Navy career.
2) Dick Cheney. A perhaps more prominent and well-known figure in politics, Cheney played a number of significant roles in US politics from the 1990s onward. Most notably, he was Vice President under George W. Bush, and Secretary of Defense for George H. W. Bush.
3) Porter Johnston Goss played his part in the George W. Bush's administration as Director of Central Intelligence and subsequently as Director of the CIA itself as well.
4) Bobby Ray Inman is yet another prominent individual in the intelligence circles of the United States. He served as the Director of the NSA from the late 1970s to early 1980s and later as the Deputy Director of Central Intelligence. The President's Intelligence Advisory Board also employed his expertise under George H. W. Bush.
5) Henry Kissinger, a man who hardly needs much introduction. Kissinger has been involved in American and global politics for a long time as a diplomat and through advisory roles, including that of the National Security Advisor. His impact on the global geopolitical stage, coupled with a number of controversies, has facilitated many conspiracy theories to crop up concerning his dealings and even allegiance.
6) Zbigniew Brzezinski is yet another alleged member with close ties to the political goings on in the US and the world. Much like Kissinger, Brzezinski is an expert in political science and geopolitics. For his skills in these fields, he has held the position of the National Security Advisor for President Carter, as well as a counselor in Lyndon Johnson's administration.
7) Richard Bowman Myers. General Myers has had an impressive career before his retirement, which has seen him appointed as the Chairman of the Joint Chiefs in the early 2000s, where he played many different advisory roles and was one of the masterminds behind

the invasion of Iraq. Furthermore, after he retired from the military, Myers was involved with a renowned defense contractor Northrop Grumman, on its board of directors. This is the corporation that has worked on several stealth aircraft projects, most notable of which is, perhaps, the B-2 Spirit bomber.
8) Sir Kevin Tebbit. Tebbit has held the highest position of civil service in the UK at one time as Permanent Undersecretary of Defense. His career is a long stretch of involvement with the British government, the Ministry of Defence, NATO during the Cold War, as well as the nuclear forces in the UK armed forces.
9) The only female on the list is Carol Thatcher, the daughter of the renowned UK Prime Minister Margaret. Through being a journalist and author, she went on a different path than her mother, at least as far as the public is concerned.
10) Alan Greenspan, a renowned economist and former longtime Chairman of the Federal Reserve, which is often the object of various conspiracy theories in itself.
11) Harold Varmus is the scientist of the alleged clandestine committee. He is a highly acclaimed, Nobel Prize-winning expert in the field of medicine and has also served as the Director of the National Cancer Institute.
12) John E. Kelly III, who is one of the most notable names in the IBM Corporation. He is a Senior Vice President and Director of Research in the company.

It's important to note that this is the only document that has ever appeared as proof of the Majestic 12 and evidence of these people's involvement. Documents were handed over by Garner to serve as irrefutable evidence that what he spoke is true. Of course, the validity of these documents is still under review, and it is, perhaps, impossible for us to decide whether or not they are genuine. And even if we were able, that might be dangerous.

Most importantly, if these documents are, indeed, real, and if they demonstrate what I think they demonstrate, then this is an extraordinary breakthrough that cannot be underestimated. If this ends up being true, what else are they hiding from us? What other shadowy government figures are hiding in plain sight? What secrets are being kept from the general public? Bringing proof of the Majestic 12's existence and nominating these people is crucial – not only because it allows us to speculate, but because it can prove to be the detail we needed to crack open decades of hidden history.

Suddenly, the stories of Area 51, S4, and the alien helper, J-Rod, are no longer silly recounting of senile old men or people who are lying for attention. While it's healthy to doubt any conspiracy theory and take it with a significant grain of salt, if even a tiny part of it turns out to be real, then the truth will all unravel. If one falls, they all do, and you and I could be standing in front of one of the most important moments in history – the moment when the secrets started spilling and the secret government was uncovered.

Chapter 8: Ancient Aliens

In this chapter, you will learn:

- What ancient aliens are
- In what ways aliens might have facilitated or accelerated human development

A bold claim

Over the last few years, an interesting phenomenon has been gaining more and more traction. People are starting to explain mysteries in our history through the presence of aliens. Ancient aliens. If you back in history and look, there are dozens of examples of things we still don't understand. From monumental buildings that were erected with rudimentary technology to exceptionally intelligent people who have come up with some of our civilization's greatest inventions, a lot of stuff just doesn't add up. Let me put it like this: if you were watching a movie about the human civilization, you would be shouting "No way!" two, three times per hour. Certain things just wouldn't seem realistic, especially when it comes to sudden knowledge we seem to have happened upon.

For example, da Vinci disappeared for years with no records accounting for his absence. Upon coming back, he started churning out his many famous inventions, including his flying machine, parachute, helicopter, scuba gear, clock, and many others. He is often said to be a man "ahead of his time," and perhaps that is precisely what we should be suspicious of. Was he just incredibly and inexplicably multi-talented and a genius, or did he receive some help literally from ahead of his time?

These strange aspects of history have prompted people, including scientists, to dig deeper, consider the issue from multiple points of view and come up with some theories as to what could be the possible explanation. The conclusion many of them landed on may surprise you or even shock you if you are unfamiliar with it. But once you take the time to think about it, you will see that it makes perfect sense: some of our greatest achievements and the furthering of technology, in particular, was facilitated by the involvement of supremely intelligent extraterrestrial beings.

Are you surprised? Perhaps you are, and your mind is blown, or maybe you're sitting there thinking "Yes, this makes sense!" Perhaps you've had a sudden revelation today. I remember when I first heard about this concept, I laughed it off and dismissed it entirely. I mean, ancient aliens? Yeah, sure! But then, the more I thought about it, the more it made sense. *Of course,* we had to have help from somewhere outside of our realm. That would explain why we had periods of fast development and rapidly emerging technology, while the rest of the time, we more or less stagnated. Especially when you take into account various techniques and mechanics of the ancient world, there is almost no other explanation at all, much less a better one.

Incredible structures

The most obvious example I can give you is the pyramids. It is the year 2015, and we, as a species, as a society, as intelligent, educated, informed beings capable of remarkable thinking and with access to incredibly detailed research and history, can still not "crack the code", so to speak, when it comes to the way these pyramids were built. Sure, there has been speculation, and every once in a while, an Egyptologist or someone comes forward with some new theory on how, exactly, the Egyptians were able to build such magnificent structures with such rudimentary means. Some say they just had a lot of slaves, others suppose it just took hundreds of years to build them, while others are convinced that they applied advanced mathematical and physics principles that we have yet to discover.

But among the wild speculation, there's this theory of alien activity; and it makes sense. Not only would it explain the actual building of these structures, but it also provides an explanation for some of the hieroglyphics found on the walls. Egyptian representations of large light bulbs, people with abnormally large and oblong heads, and even plane and spaceships have baffled people for years, and now we may have found the reason and the logic behind them. Aliens visited Earth and lent a hand to Egyptians.

Egypt is not the only place that benefited from special alien treatment, either. There are hundreds of structures around the world that would have been near-impossible to build, given the technology available at the time or that display strange signs, symbols, and drawings that could indicate extraterrestrial intervention. Take Stonehenge, for example – we don't know how those giant blocks got where they are.

There have been many guesses regarding its purpose and the way it was built, but none of them have actually become a sound conclusion. While most agree that it was some kind of temple, we have no idea how the massive stone blocks were not only stacked upon one another, but also transported there. That's right, it appears that the materials required were not even in the area, so they must have brought them from somewhere else; but how? They are giant and cumbersome, and the technology was not stellar.

The same goes for several other structures in the world; cases, where the materials used for their building, seems to have been brought all the way from a different continent, which would have required them to be transported over the ocean. However, it would have been impossible to do so, due to their incredible weight and size. What is more, many of these structures or parts of them are perfect in shape or size. They are carefully cut and assembled, and there are no imperfections in sight. Now, these structures being impossible to build at the time is one thing, but the real shock factor here is that many of them are impossible – or at least exceptionally difficult, time-consuming and expensive – to build even today, with all of our intelligence, development, and apparently superior technology.

Another unusual megalithic structure that puzzles the mind has to be the Saksaywaman fortress in Peru. Parts of it were first built by the Killke sometime around the 12th century, with significant additions put in later by the Incas, as this was close to their historic capital city. The fortress, or citadel, consists of massive stone walls, which incorporate enormous stones that can weigh up to a couple of hundred tons. The way that these stones were cut to fit so flawlessly into each other has been troubling archaeologists for a long time. What's even more bewildering is that the individual boulders are so variable in shape and size, yet they are all cut in a way that makes them fit on top and to the sides of each other seamlessly and so tightly that it is said that not even a razor can fit between them.

What happened?

So, then, how is this possible? As the theory goes, aliens visited Earth and helped humankind by lending them from their technology. Some people believe these were ancient aliens – proof of their vastly superior intelligence, even at that time – while some believe that they were aliens who came from the future. Another theory is that they were not aliens, but humans coming from the future or even from other planets we would have since populated. Obviously, no one can know for sure, but the subject definitely lends itself to speculation.

This particular supposition is maybe stronger than others, precisely because it would explain so many things, including the extraordinary intelligence of people like Da Vinci or Michelangelo, for example, but also several instances of tribes having representations of "Gods" descending from the heavens. There are drawings, symbols, and rituals illustrating this particular act of coming to Earth from somewhere up above. Sometimes, wings or fire are involved. In fact, some of these same representations appear even in the Bible, under the guise of angels appearing to mortals. The tongues of fire that accompany their descent or the wings they have could easily be future or extraterrestrial technology.

Chapter 9: Religion and Aliens

In this chapter, you will learn:

- What aliens have to do with religion
- Why aliens could be the answer to burning questions about ancient civilizations

A bit about ancient spirituality

Before going any further, you should know that there are also various current religions that not only acknowledge the existence of aliens and UFOs, but they actually regard them as their central elements of belief. They are called UFO religions, and some of the most popular are Raëlism, Nation of Islam, Heaven's Gate and Aetherius Society. However, the world's largest and most famous UFO religion is Scientology, created by L. Ron Hubbard, an SF author (no wonder, huh?).

Now, going back to ancient spirituality. One of the most fascinating aspects of the question of alien existence is definitely the ties it has with religion and spirituality, particularly in ancient civilizations. While there is currently no mainstream belief system that ascribes deity characteristics to extraterrestrials, there has been a lot of talk about ancient religions and who these people were actually praying to. It's not just the fundamental doubt of who these entities were, but also other things, such as representations, depictions, descriptions, as well as knowledge and "coincidences" that are anything, but coincidental.

Ancient spirituality was largely polytheistic, which means they believed in and prayed to several gods, as opposed to just one, as the monotheistic religions of today. They generally ascribed weather behavior and natural disasters to the wrath or mercy of their gods, who – very interestingly – always seem to reside in the sky. Most representations of a deity will show them either descending from the heavens or overseeing things from high up.

Now, this has a few explanations. One of them is related to the weather I mentioned earlier – weather was long interpreted as a sign of a deity's feelings or intentions; the weather was "sent" by God. Another thing is that for a ruler to supposedly see all, it would make sense for them to be somewhere up above, controlling their people and their land.

Bowing down to extraterrestrials

Of course, we could spend hours discussing it, and this is by no means a detailed explanation or exploration of the conventional interpretation of ancient spirituality. That's because I want to offer an alternative explanation that is by no means widely accepted, but which makes so much sense. Have you ever considered the possibility that all the depictions of gods descending from heavens are actually aliens?

I know it *sounds* crazy, but think about it for a second – they would fit the description of the enlightened being who has come to Earth. They come from "the heavens," they fly or float, they are vaguely humanoid, and they would have powers that no one on Earth, particularly in that time, would have. Other theories suggest that these revered figures could even be other humans who came from the future, either from Earth or other planets. This explanation would also "tick" all the imaginary boxes I listed above.

Even if you think that it's improbable and that it's a silly explanation, consider something else: there have been several instances of ancient civilizations having the knowledge they shouldn't have – and couldn't have – had. Let's take awareness of the universe, the planets, the stars, constellations, etc. The Hindu religion bases a lot on astrology and the knowledge of planets and their location, but how would Ancient Indians figure this out? The pyramids in Egypt have been discovered to be built according to some very specific coordinates – again, vastly superior knowledge, considering the time period.

Then, let's take the statues and drawings ancient civilizations have of their gods. Many of them – Mayan statues come to mind – look strikingly like something that resembles a human, but not necessarily. They sometimes also have helmets, hats or oblong heads, in the case of some Egyptian drawings. Of course, interpretations are many, and it's difficult to pinpoint what the "right" one is, but you have to stop and consider the possibilities, here. Everything we thought we knew might turn out to have been totally bogus, and this can very well be the explanation.

There are too many common elements and themes that appear as the same in very different parts of the world, at the same time. What is the possibility that every civilization on Earth developed in the same way? That they worshiped similar "gods"? Is an extraterrestrial visit the more logical explanation or, the crazier one? The possibilities are varied and numerous and because of that, and our limited insight, it is close to impossible to be able to tell what is fact and what is fiction.

Sure, it's possible that aliens or humans from the future visited Antiquity, but it's also possible this was just the natural course of things; that this is the human imagination and the human mind at work. If we were to start civilization all over again, would we come to the same conclusions of deities from the sky? Would we have the same representations? Or would we need to be influenced by an extraordinary occurrence in order for us to introduce this kind of mythology in the history of humankind?

The subject is fascinating and lends itself to much debating, but who can tell what the truth is? How can we possibly determine what happened thousands of years ago and whether their gods were real or not when we don't yet know the truth about the gods we worship today? The fact of the matter is that our general understanding of God still comes from the sky, and it still rules us with superior and omniscient knowledge. He still sees all and knows all, much like ancient gods. Is this a hold-over from back then? Are the echoes of an alien encounter still felt today?

Until we get some conclusive evidence, these are not questions I can answer; or anyone else, for that matter. For the time being, these remain fascinating questions about human civilization, human evolution, and human psychology. Not to mention the possibility of a close encounter of the third kind. Until then, we are left with questions and mysteries. Who built the pyramids? How? Under who's guidance? Who built Stonehenge and how? Who built the giant statues on Easter Island? What are they meant to represent? Why are they so massive and why were only the heads visible? Were they modeled after giant aliens?

Intelligent design – Abrahamic God or aliens?

An even more controversial theory that we can relate to aliens is the very concept of intelligent design. The vast majority of religious folks and believers currently in existence are convinced that the human race was born with the help of something we call "intelligent design" – in other words, that God made the human being and put him on earth. It's the same explanation used for the creation of the universe, including our planet, with everything it holds, from plants to animals and everything in between.

The reasoning behind this is simple enough: our world is created so perfectly, so symmetrically, and works together so seamlessly, that it's hard to imagine that someone *didn't* think it up. And although it is widely known that the universe was formed when the Big Bang happened and that humans, in their current form, are the products of evolution, some find it hard to believe. Furthermore, an argument in favor of the intelligent design theory is that it is not necessary to reject the

Big Bang theory or even evolution because the concept of a supreme being and intelligent creator fits right in.

So, if we were to believe this, the world would have to have been carefully planned, organized, and calculated before coming into being. As I said earlier, the vast majority of people who believe in intelligent design attribute it to God (of Abrahamic religion fame), but I am going to propose a possibly shocking idea: what if intelligent design is, indeed, how we came to be, but aliens are behind it? Now, I'm certain a lot of people would call this line of reasoning blasphemous and would maybe even call for my head to fall for even daring to suggest such a thing.

However, if we are open to exploring the existence of aliens in our universe and their possible involvement in our world here, on Earth, we cannot ignore the option of aliens not only acting as "helpers" along the way but of them being the actual creators – of us and our world. Whether or not God, as we know him, is an alien, is a question that will probably forever remain unanswered, but you can't deny that there are certain aspects that fit. From the fact that God resides in the sky to his superior intelligence to the fact that he supposedly created man in his image.

Judging by all the representations of aliens we have conjured up over the years, aliens don't look like humans, but they are positively humanoid. Their body and facial features are similar, albeit differently developed to supposedly suit a different living environment. After all, everything adapts to the environment it lives in, and who says it isn't possible for humans to have started out looking like aliens, or the other way around?

The sad part is that this particular theory is going to be dismissed as the ravings of some kind of lunatic, but don't be quick to judge it so harshly; there are real, honest-to-God scientists who are open to the possibility. Not least of all Richard Dawkins, who famously supports and argues for

Darwin's Theory of Evolution – so you know he has no real interest in dismantling his own arguments.

In fact, Mr. Dawkins believes that Intelligent Alien Design and evolution are not mutually exclusive, at all. His reasoning is this – supposedly, some kind of alien life form could have come into being through a type of evolution. It is possible that these creatures advanced to a point where they were able to create new life and that somehow this new kind of life ended up on Earth, or perhaps they "planted" it here. Either way, this theory excludes us being controlled by our creator, like a God. Instead, it's more akin to being supervised or observed by our possible extraterrestrial creators.

Of course, none of these suppositions are rooted in evidence; they are merely suggestions, possibilities, and imagined scenarios. It is not outside the realm of possibility that such a thing could have happened, but until we find actual evidence that points one way or another – whether that indicates alien involvement or not – we cannot say for sure what is true and what isn't, and we cannot dismiss the possibility.

Be that as it may, I'll go over a few of the religions that I mentioned at the start of this chapter. These faiths either revolve around the belief in UFOs as their central notion or at least make a mention of their existence. While we can't answer our questions with absolute certainty, it's interesting to hear out the claims these groups make and explore their origin, as they appear to believe them with quite a conviction.

Raëlism

This is a religion that explicitly teaches that humans and other life on Earth were created by extraterrestrial beings, referred to by the worshipers by the Biblical Hebrew term Elohim. As the story goes, the Elohim are a species of highly advanced aliens who sparked life into existence on our planet and then continued to visit, interfere, and observe human progress throughout our history. The Elohim are said to look like humans, at least in their interaction with us. Raëlism also states that the Elohim deceived the early mankind into thinking that they were angels, gods, and the like, most likely in order to conceal their true nature.

The religion was founded in 1974 and is still led by French-born Claude Maurice Marcel Vorilhon, who now goes by Raël, and it is based out of Geneva, Switzerland. Raëlism also has its own kind of clergy consisting of seven levels. New arrivals who wish to follow the teachings and become members are required to denounce their current faith officially and become apostates thereof.

Despite its unique approach to explaining the intelligent design, Raëlism doesn't entirely dismiss all aspects of other religions. In particular, the mythology makes a mention of many of the prophets and prominent figures in the stories of Christianity, Buddhism, Islam, and others. Moses, Muhammad, Jesus Christ, and Buddha are only some of these characters. However, their role in the teachings of Raëlism is different in that it describes them as messengers or prophets of the Elohim, who established contact with them and directed them to pass on their wisdom to humanity. It is one of the central beliefs of Raëlism that Raël himself is the last of these human messengers of the Elohim.

In a way, this belief stems from where the roots of the religion can be found in the first place. Starting in 1974 with one of his books, Raël claimed that he had experienced a close encounter with these alien beings and not just any kind of encounter. He said that he communicated with the visitors and that they gave him incredible insight and an important message. Allegedly, the Elohim explained to him just how the world's major religions came about, and they appointed him their messenger who was to inform humanity that if and when they reach a sufficient level of awareness and peace, the Elohim would return to be greeted by their creation – humanity.

As you can tell, that's quite a claim, and it would mark Raël as a very important individual. A pessimist might say that this condition that the Elohim have set for humanity is rather convenient for Raël's narrative too. Why? Well, a "level of awareness and peace" that would satisfy our supposed creators is quite an ambiguous goal to set, and who's to say that humanity will ever achieve this, to any degree? It's safe to assume that, according to this story, it would be left up to Raël to determine how far humanity must develop in order to be honored once again by the presence of the Elohim. Apart from that, the knowledge that he alleges was given unto him would also make him something of an authority on the validity of all the world's religions. Disregarding these high claims and how we may feel about them, this is not where the beliefs of Raëlism end.

It's important to note that the nature of Raëlian beliefs mostly steers clear of the supernatural, denying the existence of anything like the soul or a supernatural deity, and instead leans towards the scientific. The creation of life on Earth was thus carried out by the Elohim through means of science, which means genetic engineering in particular. Raëlians also believe that humans too will be able to create life on other planets one day in this way as well, but only after they have surpassed their violent ways and moved into a new era of harmony and prosperity, which would allow technology and science to flourish like never before.

These beliefs profoundly impact and shape the sociopolitical views and activism of the religion. Most notably, the adherents of the Raëlian Religion are therefore strongly in favor of things like genetically engineered foods (GMO) and human cloning, which they believe, is the answer for homosexual couples and those who can't have children due to infertility. They also believe that cloning, coupled with mastering the possibility of mind transplantation, can allow humans in the future to permanently acquire a brand new body if their natural one has a disease or is otherwise compromised.

Another interesting aspect of this religion is the story of Raël's close encounter as well. He alleges that it occurred in 1973 when he stumbled upon a UFO at the Puy de Lassolas volcano in the Auvergne region of France. He described the craft's shape as resembling a flattened bell. He then met with the occupant, who was a 25,000-year-old alien who interestingly enough was called Yahweh. Yahweh looked like a human, and he explained to Raël all about the Elohim and the *true* story of creation on Earth. His story offered answers that revealed the true nature of many of the Bible's stories as well. The Garden of Eden was therefore described as an Elohim laboratory, Noah's Ark was a spacecraft used to store DNA, and the Great Flood was actually a result of a nuclear explosion caused by the Elohim.

Heaven's Gate

If you haven't heard of this religious group by name, you may have heard of an incident in 1997 where the police in San Diego came upon a scene of what appeared to be ritualistic mass suicide, with the bodies of thirty-nine people confirmed on site. These were the members of the Heaven's Gate cult. Their infamous undertaking caused quite a stir back in the day and was widely covered by the mainstream media.

Needless to say, this is a religious group that since does not exist, but its roots go back to the early '70s, with the religion's establishment finalized in 1974. This UFO religion was founded and led by Marshall Applewhite and Bonnie Nettles, with the latter dying of cancer in 1985, twelve years before the cult's gruesome end. Although the religion itself is long gone, Heaven's Gate still stands as a grave reminder of just how dangerous cults can be. What's also interesting is the base belief system that the religion is based upon and that played a crucial role in the voluntary death of its thirty-nine members.

It all started in 1972 when Applewhite met Nettles who was very intrigued by biblical prophecies and the occult and would become his very close friend. The seed of their religion itself was probably in her claims that alien visitors foretold their meeting to her prior to their encounter. She also *informed* Appleworth that he had an all-important divine task to fulfill. This was only the starting point of the lengths their beliefs stretched to, though.

A theory soon developed in their minds that they were the chosen ones who were to bring the biblical prophecies to life while being blessed with minds far more developed than those of other people. They went as far as to suggest that Appleworth may be a reincarnation of Jesus himself. Their faith further professed that the two were to be killed and would then come back to life. Then, others would witness their ascent onto an alien spaceship, much like Jesus ascended into heaven upon his resurrection. This belief that directly involved death is likely what laid the foundation for the subsequent tragedy in 1997. Soon after their religion began to morph into a solid whole, the two began to seek out followers of the dogma and decided to attempt to establish contact with their alien overlords. At the meetings they would host for their supporters and would-be followers, they informed everybody that they were the representatives of these alien beings here on Earth. The extraterrestrial supreme beings were, according to the two, seeking volunteers for an important experiment, for which the participants would be awarded an evolutionary boost.

The teachings of the Heaven's Gate religion also incorporated an imminent cataclysm scenario, which was paramount for the Dogma. Namely, they believed that a great recycling or renewal of the Earth was coming in the near future, which would pose a certain threat to human civilization. They believed that the only way to survive this apocalypse was to actually leave the Earth and join the Next Level. The first step towards achieving this was to sever all connection to what is a typical human life within society. This meant family ties, relationships, material possessions including money, sexuality, and their very individuality or identity. Accordingly, the human body was considered and often referred to merely as a "vehicle," which served the simple purpose of facilitating this journey. Also interesting, considering what happened later, is the Heaven's Gate's take on suicide. In particular, they were against it, but they defined it somewhat differently than what is common. For them, suicide simply meant refusing the Next Level when it is offered.

Already, you can see that physical, Earthly life, as we know it, was hardly a priority in the teachings of Heaven's Gate, and it gets even wilder. The goal was reaching the Next Level and something that the adherents referred to as The Evolutionary Level above Human, or TELAH. Although it sounds primarily like a state of being, TELAH was envisioned as both a physical and a spiritual place in the cosmos. It was said to be an environment where creatures lived in a utopia, freed of all that reduces them to mere mammals, including the need for nutrition, reproduction, and even death itself.

The faith of Heaven's Gate also made mentions of a different species of extraterrestrials too, who were evil and named Luciferians. These aliens deceived humans into believing they were the traditional God in order to hinder human progress and evolution. They were alleged to be highly developed and technologically advanced, possessing spacecraft, means of traveling through time, telepathy, and long lifespans. The dogma of Heaven's Gate also stated that they created many of the miracles mentioned by mainstream religions with technology such as holograms. These Luciferians were, therefore, responsible for the corruption of all faiths ever created by humans.

Finally, in March of 1997, Applewhite recorded a tape for his followers, as he did multiple times before. He spoke of the passing Comet Hale-Bopp and a spaceship that was following in its path. This spaceship was the one that the followers had to board in order to evacuate from Earth and reach beyond. According to him, the only way of boarding the ship was to leave one's vehicle, which, of course, meant committing suicide. This alien craft would then collect their souls and transport them to TELAH.

All thirty-nine members of the cult, which included Applewhite himself, proceeded to drink a poisonous mixture and put plastic bags over their heads as to ensure death. They all laid down in their bunks after this and passed away. The police found them all dressed in black, each with a purple cloth covering their heads and upper bodies. Whether their souls were evacuated by the passing spacecraft remains unconfirmed.

Aetherius Society

In some regards, particularly concerning its formation, the Aetherius Society is not unlike Raëlism. Or rather, it's the other way around, since the Aetherius Society is older, being incepted in 1955. The founder of this religion, George King, also claimed that he had direct contact with otherworldly beings, much like Raël. He described these alien beings as being so-called Cosmic Masters, who relayed to him some very important messages for humanity.

King came from a Christian background and had a profound interest in the occult and yoga practices. He claimed that the yoga expertise given unto him by a certain Swami unlocked within his mind telepathic powers, which further improved his ability to communicate with extraterrestrials. As the story goes, King's first supposed contact occurred a week before the mysterious yoga master visited his apartment. Namely, he spoke of a voice that told him, in 1954, that he was to be the voice of an interplanetary parliament here on Earth, and that he should thus prepare and act accordingly. One of the Cosmic Masters with whom King claimed to have communicated was called Aetherius, a supreme alien being living on Venus, while he alleged to have established contact with Cosmic Masters from other parts as well.

The beliefs of the Aetherius Society are variable, interesting, and also offer supposed explanations for some of the questions concerning UFOs and similar matters. The teachings incorporate aspects of some mainstream religions such as Christianity, Buddhism, and Hinduism, combining them with the UFO phenomenon and yoga. The religion focuses heavily on spirituality and also touches upon karma and spiritual or religious healing, with an emphasis on the power of prayer. Furthermore, the Aetherius Society makes mentions of prominent figures and deities from other religions, such as Jesus, Buddha, and Krishna. However, according to their teachings, these are simply other Cosmic Masters who descended upon the Earth from other planets with the aim of elevating human spirituality and teaching the ways of proper life. Jesus and Buddha are said to be Venusians, while Krishna came from Saturn.

These Masters, or Avatars as the adherents refer to them, do not exist in the mere physical form like we do, though. The Aetherius Society explains their state of being as a primarily spiritual one, elevated to a whole new dimension of existing. The religion claims that the Cosmic Masters achieve this level of existence by maintaining what they call a higher vibratory rate. They further explain that this rate can be altered to a lower frequency, which makes the beings, as well as UFOs, visible to mere humans as well.

Apart from the Cosmic Masters, the Aetherius Society teaches of the existence of other alien forces in the universe, which are evil and have malicious intent towards the Earth. It's further suggested that the Cosmic Masters are what stands in their way and that they have fended off numerous attempted attacks from these hostile forces in many cosmic battles. However, it is the belief of this religion that the greatest peril for humanity stems from what they call the spiritual energy crisis, which has plagued humans for a long time. The Aetherius Society holds a number of sociopolitical stances, acknowledges various issues facing human civilization, and has activated itself in efforts against pollution, for example. Still, it is the belief of this religion that all of our problems will be resolved once the greater spiritual crisis that plagues the Earth is overcome.

You may get the impression, and perhaps rightly so, that the Aetherius Society is primarily humanitarian and not malicious, as can be said for the Heaven's Gate, for example. This is mainly because of the focus of their teachings on benevolent Cosmic Masters and the ways in which they help humans strive for greatness and improve themselves. That kind of attitude in faith points to an interest in improving life here on Earth, instead of escaping the imminent cataclysm and saving one's self. This is corroborated by what the religion officially claims as their goals too. The whole dogma revolves around one central effort, and that is the improvement of cooperation between the Cosmic Masters and us, in turn bolstering our spirituality. All this is pursued with the aim of avoiding a catastrophe on our planet, which we can all agree may indeed come from a number of sources.

Ultimately, the Aetherius Society is still merely a religion, and a New Age one at that. This means that it promotes alternative medicine and unproven methods of healing, and also focuses heavily on prayer, which it claims can prevent disastrous events through psychic power. I'll leave it up to you to determine how you feel about that, but it is my impression that, if nothing else, at least the intention is well-meaning. Finally, the Aetherius Society believes that one of its assignments on Earth is to facilitate the arrival of the next Cosmic Master who will land in his alien spacecraft to make his power known and represent the other Masters as well, one of which is now George King himself until his death in the late 1990s.

The Nation of Islam

The nation of Islam, or NOI, is a fairly controversial religious movement that started out in 1930 when it was established by the rather mysterious Wallace Fard Muhammad in Detroit.

The man was born in Afghanistan and came to America in the aforementioned year when he began teaching his unique form of Islam to the local African Americans. Little was discovered about his background, and he was known to use aliases. Not too long after his arrival, Wallace just disappeared in 1934 and was never seen again. This left the leadership to Elijah Muhammad who was succeeded by his son Warith in 1975, who was cast aside by Louis Farrakhan in 1977.

Now, while the Nation of Islam can technically be classified as a UFO religion, the UFO phenomenon is hardly central to its teachings. The religion merely acknowledges their existence and makes a few mentions of UFOs, which is enough to classify it. Still, the religion has had some quite peculiar moments and has come out with a number of wacky theories, some of which border science fiction.

As far as their take on UFOs goes, Elijah Muhammad taught the adherents of the religion about their existence. More precisely, he made references to the Book of Ezekiel (1:15-18), in which, he describes, Ezekiel observed a 'Mother Plane or Wheel,' which was actually a UFO. Some other theorists, particularly ancient astronaut theorists, have also been on the record saying that this was a UFO, also pointing to the famous illustration of Ezekiel's vision of the glowing wheel in the sky. Farrakhan continued with the acknowledgment of the UFOs under his leadership as well, citing Elijah and explaining that "UFO" was the way white people refer to them. Furthermore, he went on to claim that the wheel came from Japan. The Nation of Islam, therefore, widely believes that UFOs originate from Japan.

If you think that's weird, wait until you hear their views on the origins of different races in the world, and you'll begin to learn some really wacky stuff, as well as start to understand the criticism that this group has received over the decades a little better.

The Nation of Islam's teachings concerning race were first established by Wallace Fard Muhammad himself. As the mythos goes, the Black or African people were the first and only people on Earth for a time. This was until an evil scientist by the name of Yakub, or Jacob in the Holy Bible and the Quran created the white man through a unique form of birth control and engineering. Fard claimed that the scientist Yakub carried out his undertaking on Patmos, a Greek island, and instilled into the whites a culture that revolved around deception and killing, which is why Fard referred to them as a race of "devils." It took around six hundred years to breed the white race into the one of blonde hair and blue eyes. Making matters even worse, while this breeding process was coming along, Yakub's race had clandestine plans and conspiracies to murder the offspring of all the black people in order to hinder their birth rate. They also segregated themselves to preserve their purity and worked towards establishing a system that favored the whites in all aspects of life and society.

Once the new, white race was in full swing, it began to migrate to mainland Europe first, inflicting all manner of misery upon the friendly indigenous people who welcomed them with open arms. This is, more or less, expressed in the supreme wisdom lessons of the Nation of Islam as the root cause of actual historical injustices such as colonialism, slavery, etc.

Some members of the NOI have targeted other races and religious groups as well, blaming Jews for purposely inventing slavery in order to hurt black people. Others have even accused Jewish scientists of developing HIV and infecting Black people with it in order to kill them with AIDS. Granted, the proponents of these theories usually speak on their own, and it's noteworthy that Farrakhan personally denied the allegations of the NOI being anti-Semitic, stating in his defense that those who come out with these accusations are simply looking to silence legitimate criticism of Zionism and the political establishment in Israel.

Besides racism, hate, and xenophobia, some critics have gone after the Nation of Islam in the past for their many discrepancies with the traditional teachings of both Sunni and Shia Islam, questioning the legitimacy of their name itself. This kind of grievance was also the one held by the famous Malcolm X, who was a prominent member of the NOI in his time, before leaving the organization to convert to the traditional Sunni Islam. As you may or may not know, Malcolm X was killed by members of the Nation in 1965.

The Nation of Islam has also recently been criticized for growing ever closer to the Church of Scientology, with Farrakhan engaging many of his followers to take up the study of Dianetics.

Scientology – the most famous UFO religion

When I say "Scientology," you say "Tom Cruise"! No, seriously now, Scientology is currently best known as the wacky religion of Hollywood celebrities, most famous of which is Tom Cruise and his couch-jumping self. Unless you've been part of this cult or have had personal experience of some sort, you probably don't know much about it, except for the stories that get bandied about in gossip magazines.

"Tom Cruise's wife was forced to endure a silent birth!", "Scientologists don't believe in mental illness," "Scientology is a pyramid scheme" – these are just a few of the snippets of reality filtered through the public eye. But instead of talking about crazy, wealthy celebrities and their preferred religion of the week (anyone remember Kabbalah?), I'm going to tell you some actual facts about Scientology, instead. And then, I'm gonna touch upon its relation to aliens and why it's categorized as a UFO religion.

First things first – Scientology was created as recently as 1954 by L. Ron Hubbard. As I briefly mentioned at the beginning of this chapter, this guy was a science-fiction writer (you've gotta be, to be able to dream up an entire cult, right?) who developed what is known as Dianetics. Now, Dianetics is the belief in a relationship between the body and the mind and in a balance that is required to exist between them. Dianetics is practiced in Scientology, and it is here where the rejection of the concept of mental illness comes from.

Scientologists believe that mental illness of all kinds is a distortion, aberration, or disruption of the basic human drive for survival and goodness and that it can be "cured" through a process called "auditing." You see, Scientologists don't ascribe to the id, ego, and superego, but to the "analytical mind" (the conscious), the "reactive mind" (the subconscious), and the "somatic mind." In their understanding, the reactive mind is the one who taints the sanity of the individual and through auditing, the goal is to erase the effects of past experiences that interfere with current happiness.

Now, what about that alien business I mentioned earlier? Well, Scientology is among the UFO religions, as noted by Gregory Reece (UFO Religion: Inside Flying saucer cults and culture), Susan Palmer, James, R. Lewis (The Encyclopedic Sourcebook of UFO Religions) and Christopher Partridge (UFO Religions), because UFOs and the aliens flying them are part of the core tenets of belief.

However, Scientology is special, even among the UFO religions, because it is more secretive in nature than others. They try their hardest to hide information about space, the galactic federation, etc. Another thing to note is that the founder of Scientology, L. Ron Hubbard, presented lectures and wrote about what is known as space opera. The interesting thing is that not all Scientologists will even know about the role of cosmology within the religion – or if they know, they'll pretend they don't.

The "truths" are only for the high-ranking members of the cult, and that status is earned through cold, hard cash. Hundreds of thousands of it. That means that few people have had the "honor" of learning some of the most well-kept secrets of

Scientology. But even so, documents surfaced in the 90s, basically confirming what everyone had been whispering and supposing until then. Hubbard believed in something called the Galactic Confederacy, which was supposedly ruled by Xenu, the evil overlord, 75 million years ago.

I'm not going to go into the entire complicated story (but I urge you to go check it out because it's crazy-sounding and amazing). The short version is that the planets in the Confederacy were overpopulated, so the overflowing aliens were shipped off to Earth, where they were blown up to their death. Their souls, however, were collected by Xenu, who planted false history and beliefs and then they were left to roam or otherwise haunt the people on Earth, who are now suffering from mental distress and illness because of these souls called "thetans." In order to be rid of them, you need to – you guessed it – pay a lot of money. And I mean a LOT, especially if you want to achieve "clear" status.

There are entire books to be written not only about Scientology and its relationship with aliens and UFOs but about the other UFO religions, as well. The information is downright fascinating, and whether or not you believe it to be true or even plausible, you cannot deny how interesting it is and how remarkable that a cult was created based on the science fiction written by a guy who was looking to get rich.

I'm sorry if I'm going to let you down in the conclusion of this chapter, but the common theme here is the impossibility of knowing. I urge you to look into the matter and do more research, because the topic is incredibly interesting, and who knows? You may gain some insight. But if definite answers are what you are looking for, I'm afraid we're just going to have to wait.

Chapter 10: Unconfirmed Evidence

In this chapter, you will learn:

- What NASA is doing about extraterrestrials
- What (unofficial) evidence we have so far

Does NASA evidence support claims?

So, we've been talking about aliens and UFOs and all sorts of stories, claims and conspiracy theories, but what we haven't talked about so far is evidence or research. Does the government occupy itself with the extraterrestrial problem? Is NASA making efforts to uncover new information about it? More importantly, has NASA *already* revealed any new and relevant facts that can contribute to our understanding of alien life?

Sadly, I can't tell you that anything is confirmed. While research has been conducted and we have satellites and robots out in space, studying the soil of Mars, life has not yet been discovered. What has been found, however, is that Mars used to be habitable. It may not seem like much, but this is a massive breakthrough, considering that before this, all we had were speculations. Now we know for a fact that a planet that is so close to us may have been, at one point, populated by some sort of organism, intelligent or not.

Another thing is that various pieces of "evidence" have been analyzed over the years – remember the powder residue on Betty Hill's dress? – But the results have always been inconclusive. Even in the cases where there were various witnesses to account for the presence of a UFO or its presence was confirmed by some UFO organization or another there have been no official confirmations of alien presence or interaction. Research does not back up the abduction stories.

It's good to know that NASA is working on supplementing its efforts of looking for life on other planets and that this is something they are interested in. Contrary to what you may believe, this is not a subject that is taken lightly. The reason why official statements are not made is that they cannot afford to give information without it being 100% certain. That would be alarming the population for no reason. That doesn't mean that there aren't studies being made and research conducted behind the scenes – we just don't know about it. Area 51, anyone?

Alien hieroglyphics on Mars?

Something I do want to indicate as a possibility, however, is something else that has been found on Mars, thanks to the Curiosity Rover. Pictures have surfaced of some possible carvings on rock formations. They look like hieroglyphics: a message from a possible intelligent extraterrestrial civilization. Of course, the pictures are not at all very clear, and we can't know for sure if that actually is writing or what it says. As always, skeptics are unimpressed and claim that the writing is simply rock texture.

But the thing is that we don't know whether or not that is real writing. What if it is? Do you realize how potentially huge this is? If this one single piece of information were proven to be genuine, this would change the course of history, humanity and the way we relate to outer space. Our knowledge of an intelligent alien civilization and the discovery of their language is a total game-changer.

What makes this different than other theories and previous claims is that the evidence is provided by NASA itself. And while they have not come out with an official statement regarding the verity of these hieroglyphics, the possibilities are undeniably strong. Of course, it wouldn't be prudent or responsible for them to say that this is an alien language when the reality is that we don't know for sure yet. But it is also possible for them to know for a fact that these are real hieroglyphics, but they won't release that information to the general public before they figure out what they say, what they mean, how old they are, etc.

You can never really know the truth about these things, can you? No matter what the official statement is, there is always the possibility that they are lying and that they simply are not making the real information public at this moment. This could have something to do with the conspiracy theories related to the Majestic 12 and the New World Order, but it can also be just the simple fact of them wanting to do their research in peace and try to figure out what this all means, without the entire world harassing them about these new discoveries.

At the end of the day, there is not much we, as "civilians," can do about this. We don't have access to information unless they give it to us, and that is entirely their call. Only time can tell whether or not any of these alien claims are true or not. Until we see incontestable evidence, evidence that NASA or the government cannot attribute to some other explanation, we have no choice but to believe them or distrust them and wait for a dénouement in this fascinating case.

Alien languages – is it possible?

NASA would never give any indication that what the rover found was an actual alien language unless that was a confirmed fact. And even so, would they make that announcement? Maybe, maybe not, but the cynic in me is leaning towards "maybe not" because they would probably not want to alarm the population. The discovery of an alien language is something so massive that it would have profound and lasting effects on humanity here, on Earth. So, we can conclude that even if such a language were to be discovered, the information most likely wouldn't reach our ears.

So, then, let's take a step back from NASA and look at some other evidence. Who else has found strange symbols that could be interpreted as an alien language? Were there other such instances in history, or is that something we are more likely to see on "Futurama"? I can tell you that the subject is of interest; so much in fact, that there is a special term to call the study of it: ecolinguistics, which is also known as Astro linguistics and xenolinguistics. But it remains a speculative science, at best, because there have been no confirmed sightings of languages or even of intelligent life forms.

But even in the absence of an irrefutable example of an extraterrestrial language, the subject lends itself to debate and study. In fact, it is even present in language and linguistic programs in particular universities. The subject can be addressed and approached from different angles, including a philosophical one. Do aliens even have a written language? Perhaps it is just spoken, or maybe it's not even spoken, but communicated through facial expressions, body language, and sign language. In that case, it would be impossible for us to find any evidence, lest we encounter aliens and witness their means of communication.

In 1960, Hans Freudenthal (who is a Dutch mathematician) wrote about Lincos, a language built upon basic mathematic principles. Alexander Ollongren, in turn, described Lincos as a system of Astro linguistics that is formed on constructive logic. If we were to think about it in philosophical terms, Ludwig Wittgenstein famously said that – and I'm paraphrasing, here – we couldn't understand a lion if he were able to speak.

Why is that? Because we only give meaning to language when we use it in a community as a way of life. From here it results that a different creature from a different environment would have an entirely different language that would be impossible for us to understand. Other philosophers talked about the "conceptual schemes" the world is comprised of, which are not understandable amongst themselves.

What about other evidence?

So, we've settled that NASA is not providing any kind of proof at this time, either because they haven't found any, or because they have reasons to hide it. But that doesn't mean that other evidence hasn't been found; after all, NASA is not the only one interested in the goings-on in space and what comes from it, right? Ufologists, in particular, are perhaps even more interested in the problem of extraterrestrials and UFOs. There is such a thing as a "UFO hunter," who is a person who occupies themselves with looking for and spotting UFOs. Many of these UFOs have even been caught on video.

So, what's the verdict on evidence coming from alternative sources? Does it exist? Well, it does exist, but its verity is to be determined. Over the years, there have been many bits and pieces of a much larger puzzle, but nothing too concrete or several pieces from the same area of the puzzle, if you know what I mean. And with scattered evidence, we can't really do much or understand much from it. But alas, I'm going to talk about it, because it's still interesting and because it may help you form an opinion one way or another.

First, let's talk about one of the oldest pieces of evidence – mummified humanoid-looking, elongated skulls found in Peru. These date as far back as 300 BC and while they are similar to human skulls, the strange, elongated shape is undeniable unfamiliar. The other instance where we see this same skull shape is in Egyptian drawings. Now, previously, people have dismissed the Egyptian ones as something as simple as people wearing hats. But with the uncovering of these skulls, we're not that sure anymore, are we? Is it possible those were depictions of aliens? The shape certainly fits the description reported by supposed witnesses.

Another piece of possible evidence is glaringly obvious. In fact, it's so evident, that it stares you in the face, and it almost seems like someone planted it there as an anachronistic joke. "The Madonna with Saint Giovannino," a painting created in the 1400s, illustrates the Virgin Mary front and center. But what's that behind her? It's a man, out in the distance. And what is he doing? Well, he's staring at the sky at what appears to be an honest-to-god UFO. Don't believe me? Take a look for yourself.

However, opponents of this supposition often cite the Holy Bible itself as evidence to refute the claim. First and foremost, the background detail of a man with a dog watching a supposed UFO can be seen in a number of other similar artworks of that era. Theologians, art historians, and other experts say that this is meant to portray a particular part of the Bible that speaks of one of God's angels coming down to Earth and showing himself to shepherds in all his glowing glory. To be more precise, the part in question starts with Luke 2:8 and continues for a couple more verses in the Gospel of Luke.

The paintings that are said to incorporate these verses somewhat vary when it comes to details of the encounter, but a few common aspects weave through most of them. In particular, the shepherd is usually in the company of his dog, holding his hand up to his forehead in order to overshadow his eyes and get a better look at what's coming out of the sky. Different paintings portray the angel's appearance as emitting much more light than is the case with The Madonna painting itself. While some of the other pieces show the angel himself much more clearly than is the case here, the other elements of the story are still present, which would indeed corroborate the claim of this connection. Sometimes, there was more than one shepherd, the glowing cloud would be a little different, or the sky would tear as the angel comes forth, but many experts agree that the idea is the same behind all of the paintings.

As you can see below, however, the object in the sky is quite ambiguous on its own, and it's not hard to imagine why it begs the questions when it comes to this particular work of art.

*Image Source: https://commons.wikimedia.org/wiki/File:The_Madonna_with_Saint_Giovannino.jpg

Then, there's the issue of astronauts who say they've seen aliens or UFOs. Still, this isn't official data from NASA, and it's only a sighting claim, just like the others, but then again, it's not the same, is it? These are educated, intellectual, experienced men and women who know what they're talking about; not some Joe Nobody in Texas. Dr. Brian O'Leary, Cady Coleman, and Edgar Mitchell are just a few of those who claim to have seen something. They are also known to have spoken about the government awareness of extraterrestrials and their efforts of covering up the information.

At the end of the day, the rumors and conspiracy theories have to start from somewhere, right? They have to have a piece of truth. Perhaps most notably, Buzz Aldrin (who was aboard Apollo 11) recounts the experience he had when he was aboard the ship, and he and the crew noticed something flying right next to their aircraft. They mistakenly thought it was the detached rocket, only to be told by mission control that the piece in question was 6000 full miles away. This is the stuff you don't hear about and which is conveniently covered up.

I can't go on without talking about all the "civilian" sightings that have been going on for decades in various places around the world. Sometimes, it seems like most of them happen in the U.S.A., but research will show you that it's not true. As I indicated in a previous chapter of this book, sightings and encounters have been reported from the United Kingdom and Australia, with the addition of several other countries, most notably Russia, who has supposedly held the knowledge of extraterrestrial existence since 1969. Yes, that's right, the year of the moon landing. Coincidence? Who knows?

Ancient depictions of aliens?

Much like the supposed depictions of UFOs in medieval art, there are certain pieces of art dating back to the ancient times, which ancient alien theorists claim may provide evidence that people were indeed in contact with extraterrestrial beings as far back as a few millennia. These illustrations are usually found in cave wall artworks and similar remnants of earlier humans, some of which do seem quite peculiar in the way they depict what, essentially, humanoid forms are. There are multiple examples of these puzzling artworks, some of which are indeed quite unsettling in the way they resemble our more contemporary idea of what aliens might look like.

One example that theorists often point to would definitely have to be the so-called Wandjina petroglyphs left behind by Aborigines in Kimberly, Australia. They have estimated to date back to around four thousand years ago. Aboriginal mythology describes them as spirits that control clouds as well as rain, which would make the mythology around them similar to that of many other weather gods worshiped throughout the world and history. They are also believed, in old Aboriginal traditions, to have come from the clouds to be the creators of both the Earth and the people that inhabit it – in this case, the Aborigines. After a while of bringing the people into existence and facilitating their growth in different ways, the Wandjinas are believed to have disappeared, some of them descending into the Earth and some of them leaving for the skies. It's also believed that despite their disappearance, their influence still guides many of the natural occurrences on Earth.

You may wonder how the Wandijans are then different than countless other deities worshiped by various cultures throughout history. Well, the basis for theorizing about the possibility of the Wandjinas' extraterrestrial origins goes back to their aforementioned strange appearance in rock art. Namely, these spirits, or creatures, are depicted as having large, round heads that become narrower towards the chin area, usually having no mouth at all. Their color is bright white most of the time, and they have disproportionally big black eyes. Most of the illustrations of the Wandjinas also portray some kind of a halo around their heads, which ancient alien theorists claim may represent helmets.

What's also interesting to contemplate is the very fact that these beings are white in color, whereas the Aborigines have brown skin. This is hardly smoking gun evidence, of course, but it makes you wonder why they would paint them white of all colors. Either way, as soon as you look at the pictures of these figures, they begin speaking for themselves, and the way they so clearly resemble our popular concept of gray aliens is quite interesting indeed.

Another similar example is found all the way in the United States, left behind by the people of various Native American groups such as the Anasazi, Ute, Fremont tribes, and the archaic peoples that came before them, in the Sego Canyon, Utah. The different artworks that can be found there have accumulated over a period of eight thousand years, experts say, with additions from various tribes. These include various humanoid figures that vary in size and features, some of which are rather large. Ancient alien theories state that some of these figures may represent alien visitors that interacted with the people of the tribes in many ways over time. Once again, we have a distant culture that has no connection to the one we previously mentioned, yet some of their art portrays humanoid forms that are perplexing in many of the same ways as the Wandjinas.

Most of the strange beings are depicted as having no limbs or eyes, or rather, having hollow, empty eyes, the sockets of which lay very large on their faces. The figures are often surrounded by snakes, mysterious objects, and a lot of other things that are quite open to interpretation. And then there are some that appear to have wings coming from their backs, or what looks like small antennas protruding from their heads. The proponents of the theories about ancient alien visitors mostly point to the faces and heads of the beings, as they do indeed resemble aliens, just like the Wandjinas. However, experts and researchers in this field explain that the figures merely represent the visions and hallucinations that shamans had during their ritualistic trances, possibly induced by hallucinogens and various psychedelic substances used as part of these rituals. Of course, there is no way for us to know with absolute certainty what these ancient tribesmen were thinking when they were drawing their art, so it's likely that there will be no evidence to ascertain beyond any doubt either of the proposed explanations.

Chapter 11: What Makes the United States of America So Special?

In this chapter, you will learn:

- Possible explanations as to why USA has the highest number of reported UFO sightings
- Why most conspiracy theories, concerning aliens, in particular, revolve around the USA and the US government

Questions and early efforts

While the stories and theories are indeed not unique to America, the fact of the matter is that the USA is the one country in the world with the most UFO sightings and alleged alien contact reports and testimonies, by far. If you are anything like me, this will immediately make you ask at least a couple of questions. What is it that makes the US so attractive to our alleged visitors from outer space? Are all those sightings actually alien encounters? Are the American people too quick to jump to conclusions? How does the frequency of UFO sightings in America compare to the rest of the world? There are numerous factors to consider when we try answering these and other questions that one might have.

Now, as far as America is concerned, it's noteworthy to point out the extent of involvement by the government and other official channels in the UFO phenomenon and the investigation and reporting thereof. This is important because it has affected both the number of reported sightings and the quality of the information provided. Project Blue Book was one official undertaking and attempt at cracking the mystery, starting in 1947 when the UFO phenomenon started gaining a lot of public attention. It was mostly established and funded by the US Air Force and entailed providing support to research efforts and collecting reports from a variety of sources. A significant portion of those reports was contributed by civilian and private organizations such as the NICAP and AFPRO, which carried out their own investigations. The vast majority of the reported incidents that were observed in the coming years were said to be easily explainable either as known natural phenomena or man-made and natural objects. This consensus was finalized in the late 1960s with the Condon Report.

After close to two decades of data and report collection, the US Air Force assigned researchers from the University of Colorado to analyze those incidents that still defied explanation in 1966. Headed by Edward Condon, they studied the events in great detail and, two years later, concluded in their report that there was no substantial evidence to support the theory of alien contact and justify any further academic effort to study the UFO phenomena. Soon after that, the Condon Report itself was looked at by another group of scientists appointed by the National Academy of Sciences. This committee of thirty-seven scientists concluded that the report was sound and very scientific and they all wrote on it. Thus, the Condon Report was generally well-received by the scientific circles by large and stands as one of the most significant milestones in official UFO research. And with that, Project Blue Book met its end in 1969, when the government also essentially stopped acquiring UFO reports from the general public.

Of course, Project Blue Book's UFO reports database was preserved with over 12,000 alleged incidents, and it was obtained by civilian organizations such as the Center for UFO Studies, or CUFOS, which started out in 1973 and continued to look out for reported sightings, keeping its own database until 1982. CUFOS, and other private organizations like it, have kept adding to the database, which has since grown significantly. In total, there have been over 114,000 alleged sightings worldwide in the period between 1947 and 2007, around 60,000 of which have occurred in the USA.

The conclusion of Project Blue Book and the cessation of official government-funded efforts at the end of the 1960s have had a couple of very significant results that, combined with other factors, have changed a lot and ushered in a new era of UFO research. Namely, the general scientific consensus and the media's angle on the whole thing have created a significant decrease in the public's interest in the UFO phenomena, or rather the interest in finding real, concrete answers. As the science fiction sector of the entertainment industry in the 1970s began to incorporate the alien hypothesis into some of its biggest projects, the issue of UFOs morphed into material for blockbusters and literary works of fiction, instead of being a scientific quandary. This brings us to one of the possible factors that contribute to such a high number of sightings in America.

The cultural factor

We may not think about it in such terms most of the time, but a mere few things in the world are as powerful as the media and the entertainment industry, especially those of the United States. It just so happens that both of these forces were gaining incredible momentum in the second half of the 20th century, especially at the time when mainstream science and government officials began to move away from exploring the UFO phenomena and, in many people's eyes, taking a lot of the theory's credibility with them. As the scientific method wavered, creative minds of Hollywood and the like ramped up the production of movies, books, comics, and other forms of media. A lot of these creations stand to this day as some of the most fruitful and impactful works of art featuring anything from UFO sightings, over alien invasions of Earth, to pan-galactic civilizations crawling with life, technology, and species.

All of this has definitely engraved certain images into the collective consciousness of Americans and other people in the western world as well. Of course, this isn't to say that aliens have to be fiction. After all, the incidents came first, and the popular culture just followed. However, it is possible that the popularity of UFOs has contributed to more people seeing unexplained phenomena in the sky, or at least thinking that they are. When something is on our minds a lot of the time and if we also search for it with enough dedication, we are likely to see something sooner or later. The mind will strive to find that which it believes it should look for, and this is how we often convince ourselves of things that simply aren't true. And as I've said, while the industry was picking up, the science was receding, which meant that most of the speculating was now left up to creativity and everyday people who wanted to believe. It's easy to see how all this could have affected the reliability of many reports, but also further increased the sheer number of supposed encounters.

Apart from facilitating growth in the number of reported sightings, the onset of science fiction may have also settled the phenomena involving UFOs in the minds of many people, at least subconsciously, as exactly just that – science fiction. This subculture could have also prompted more people to engage in all manner of pranks, hoaxes, and scams for a range of reasons. Whether it is fame, personal amusement, or some sort of gain, it's always a possibility that people are fabricating stories, especially since the interest of the officials to investigate the reports has paled so much towards the late 20th century.

This lack of formal effort has also left the period from the late 1970s to mid-1990s as one without many breakthroughs, though the reports kept cropping up. Of course, the mid-90s saw the rise of a new form of media and communication as well – the internet. Seeing as America is the first country where the Internet began to spread rapidly, it's safe to assume that this technological breakthrough further contributed to the number of alleged UFO sightings. Expectedly, easy access to the Internet also opened the door for more reports that have very little credibility.

It definitely is a thing to consider. Hollywood and the mass media have a tremendous impact everywhere in the world, but are, of course, most potent in the United States. This has definitely created a strong subculture revolving around aliens and UFOs. Combine that with efficient means of communication, the overall high development of the country, and a significant population, and it becomes apparent how the United States is a fertile soil for these stories. However, other possible explanations and theories might shed some light on why the USA is at the center of these strange happenings. One of those is quite impressive, and its story also happens to begin the United States of America.

Nuclear proliferation

There are some people who believe that it was, in fact, our development and detonation of nuclear weapons that caught the eye of extraterrestrials and drew them to investigate just what we are doing down here. Starting with the Trinity test as part of the Manhattan Project, the US was the first country to successfully detonate a nuclear device in New Mexico, back in 1945. Being the country from which this power originates, it would be expected that any visitors who were interested in it would focus most of their investigation there. And indeed, it hasn't been uncommon for some of the most fascinating reports and sightings to emerge from areas where America's nuclear facilities and military installations are located. Military bases, especially ones hosting nuclear weapons systems, have been the object of stories about alien encounters for a long time, in the US and other countries alike.

Edgar Mitchell, a man I briefly mentioned in the previous chapter, was a longtime advocate for the existence of extraterrestrials and our contact with them, and he has actually stated that they are indeed attracted by our nuclear capabilities. Mitchell was a prominent NASA astronaut and the sixth man to walk on the surface of the Moon in 1971, as part of the Apollo 14. He has been a proponent of the conspiracy theory surrounding the UFO phenomenon for years, but it was in 2015 that he stated that aliens directly intervened during the cold war in order to prevent us from going extinct. He even went as far as to claim that our extraterrestrial visitors have shot down or otherwise disabled nuclear missiles on a number of occasions. He has also stated that many of his sources came from the corridors of power in the US military, politics, as well as from the international stage. According to Mitchell, the Roswell incident was also indeed a cover up by the government to hide from the public the facts that proved the existence of aliens and their visitation. What's also interesting is another statement he gave in 2004, about a clandestine organization of high profile people actively doing research on recovered alien bodies and working to conceal the facts. This allegation sounds an awful lot like the supposed Majestic 12, described by Ron Garner and others. Needless to say, official NASA spokespeople have respectfully denied Mitchell's theories and professed their disagreement. Edgar Mitchell was not the only one to make these claims, though.

In late September of 2010, a press conference was held in Washington D.C. at the National Press Club. Robert Hastings, a UFO author, hosted the conference with six former airmen and another military man, who all had some rather interesting things to say. They argued that the US Air Force had in-depth knowledge of the existence of extraterrestrials and was putting a lot of effort into covering it up. The men also said that these extraterrestrial visitors are the ones to thank for humanity's evasion of a nuclear exchange during the Cold War and that they quickly took an interest in our affairs when the atomic tests started out.

At this conference, the stories of UFOs disabling nuclear weapons were also told, much like the ones described by Edgar

Mitchell. Among those present was also a Colonel Charles Halt, who testified to seeing an unidentified craft in the UK as well. More precisely, at what used to be a Royal Air Force base called Bentwaters, some thirty years earlier. An interesting thing to note is that Bentwaters was one in a string of airbases in the UK where there were reports of UFO incidents back in 1956. These sightings were covered in the Condon Report, which we mentioned earlier. Things get a whole lot more interesting when you learn that the Condon Report itself didn't rule out the possibility of genuine UFOs showing up at those airbases. With all the certainty with which the Condon Committee proclaimed that the UFO phenomenon was a low concern, these particular sightings were among those unexplained. The report stated that natural explanations are not to be ruled out, although they are unlikely, while the chances of this being an actual UFO encounter "appeared to be fairly high."

If you feel that there is some merit to these theories, you may be able to see how they could be a factor in the high number of UFO encounters in the US. Of course, America is not the lone nuclear power and hasn't been one since 1949 when the USSR joined the race. However, there are two ways in which America stands out among the rest. And those are the fact that it was the American soil where nuclear power came to life for the first time and the sheer number of nuclear detonations through testing, which is over a thousand by 1992. For comparison, the next most active tester, the Soviet Union, has recorded a little over seven hundred such exercises. Of course, the US military has also detonated devices on the Pacific Proving Grounds and elsewhere in the world, but the concentration of the tests is the highest on its own mainland territory, particularly on the Nevada Test Site.

However likely or unlikely this scenario may seem to you, the fact is that many people, a lot of whom were close to the US military and the government, have come forward over the years to claim that the US is withholding crucial information.

Whether they are indeed hiding something or not, we may never find out for certain if a concerned band of extraterrestrial visitors had saved us from ourselves.

The usual suspects

Despite the fact that UFO sightings have been reported almost everywhere in the world, the US government seems to get the most flak for conspiring to hide the truth. And even though many other governments, especially that of the Soviet Union, were known for their secrecy and schemes, you will still find that most stories, whether from real life or from works of fiction, will involve a particular UFO incident and the US government working tirelessly to silence whistleblowers and bury the truth. This begs the question of why that's the case.

It is a question of how much this reality is based on hidden truth and how much it stems from culture. Casting aside the things we cannot see, it's very likely that, once again, the vibrant UFO subculture in the US contributes a great deal to the overall perception. It can even be said that there is a sort of trend to doubt and question the US government, not only when it comes to their response to the UFO phenomenon, but in many other affairs as well. And to be fair, the US has quite a track record of covert dealings throughout the world and at home, and every once in a while, the truth gets out. There have been countless conspiracy theories revolving around the US government through the decades, and a noticeable share of them has actually turned out to be true!

Take Project MKUltra for example, the secret string of mind control experiments perpetrated by the CIA on subjects who were not so willing and consenting at times, transgressing into illegality. For a long time, the existence of this project was denied, but in the end, it finally came to light and is now an admitted fact. The Gulf of Tonkin incidents in 1964 is another example. Decades later, it has been found and confirmed that the first clash with North Vietnamese patrols was, in fact, started by US forces, while the second incident didn't even happen. And yet, this supposed confrontation served as a pretext for the Gulf of Tonkin Resolution, ultimately leading to the American involvement in the brutal and costly War in Vietnam.

This is just a glimpse into the conspiracy theories that became a reality over time. So, the combination of the UFO subculture with the US government's history of various cover-ups can definitely be considered as a factor contributing to this reputation. The fact that the USA has been a very globally involved superpower for over seventy years doesn't help alleviate the suspicions either.

Now, it's important to examine another possible cause of the US being perceived as the likely conspirator. We have to cut America some slack and acknowledge that it is a highly developed country with a society that enjoys a lot of freedom, which has severely lacked in the opposing Eastern Bloc during the Cold War. This means a number of important things that contribute to people telling stories and theorizing. Firstly, America has had a very advanced and comparatively free media network for a long time, with free enterprises and stations disseminating information with little to no restriction. Coupled with the constitutionally guaranteed freedom of speech, this allowed for a lot of public debate, to which essentially anybody could contribute. In contrast, we have to consider how controlled the media and the entertainment industry were in places like the Soviet Union. Say what you want about the US of A, but while citizen assassination or imprisonment as a form of silencing dissent is a thing of speculation here, it wasn't a far stretch of the imagination in the USSR. Such governments are known to have been far more repressive, and when it came to keeping state secrets, their toolbox was well equipped with deportations, gulags, and yes, even murder. What I'm getting at is that these things, even if they may have happened in some form, would have been an outrage in the Western World, while the situation was a lot different in much of the rest of the world.

The main difference here is that the US government, while attempting to keep secrets, would utilize media manipulation and strong and absolute denial of all accusations, still leaving people free to talk and speculate as they please. The communist countries were not hesitant to use actual force when it came to these issues. This is likely the reason that there are fewer UFO reports and conspiracy theories in some locations. That doesn't mean, of course, that they have any less to hide than the US does.

So there you have it, an open and relatively free society has the freedom to run as wild as it pleases with speculation. That means a lot of junk in the information pool, but this is not a big problem as long as the scientific method is applied. Some unexplained phenomena, a possible grain of truth that lies dormant, and a lot of public discourse are likely to produce a broad range of interesting stories and theories over decades, stories which, naturally, end up mostly revolving around the government of the country in question.

Chapter 12: Rare Natural Phenomena, Aliens, or Something Else?

In this chapter, you will learn:

- Examples of peculiar phenomena in nature that defy explanation
- Theories and attempts to explain them

Before we get to exploring a few of these strange occurrences, I should say that I am, of course, not implying they necessarily have to do with aliens, though such theories do exist in most cases. The mysterious nature of these phenomena and the lack of any concrete explanations leave a lot of room for speculation, and where there is no scientific answer, a few things are beyond the realm of the possible.

Ultimately, it is up to each individual to look at the information and decide for themselves whether the official evidence and answers are sufficient to settle the mystery.

The trumpet of the Apocalypse

When we think of mind-boggling mysteries of nature, we usually think of things we'd be able to see but can't explain. However, the phenomenon I'm about to discuss cannot be visually observed, and it is intangible, for you see, it is simply a sound.

Starting less than a decade ago, more and more people from different parts all over the world have been reporting an unusual, loud noise that seems to emanate straight from the sky without warning and apparent explanation. Russia, the US, Ukraine, Poland, Germany, Indonesia, the Philippines, and Belarus are only some of the countries from which reports have come in over the years, amounting to thousands of people since 2011. Thanks to widespread access to smart gadgets and the Internet, this is one of the most documented phenomena of our lifetimes. There are video and audio recordings in great abundance all over the Internet, available for everyone to see and examine. What's particularly strange is that it appears that this sound was not recorded before and seems to be a phenomenon of our time. While some videos are possibly hoaxes, the possibility of the phenomenon itself being a hoax is long gone, in part due to a significant number of witnesses from all corners of the globe, but also because NASA has officially acknowledged the sound as real.

This ominous racket comes without any foreshadowing and apparently at random, with no other manifestations or any consistent, discernible prelude or follow-up; the only signature of the occurrence is the sound itself. It can happen in clear and stormy weather alike, at differently elevated areas, on multiple continents, at night or in daytime. The characteristics of the particular noise are relatively universal, although they vary in intensity, sound intervals, and frequency. The best known, and probably the most unsettling form of this sound comes as a trumpet-like noise that rumbles through the skies above over and over again for an extended period. Another way to describe it is to compare it to the metallic ruckus you would expect from a colossal piece of industrial machinery as it moves across the landscape. It is a thing of film, the way it resonates through the sky all around the observer, as if straight from a science fiction scene where an enormous spaceship looms overhead and moves upwards above the camera, or a massive alien tripod from War of the Worlds stalking the battlefield. If you've seen the film, you'll know exactly what I am talking about. The way this sound resembles the alien fighting machines from the film is absolutely uncanny, to say the least!

As unbelievable as that may sound to any rational mind, the phenomenon is out there for all to hear, and nobody can describe it as well as it can describe itself. So, I highly suggest you do an Internet search, and you will immediately be bombarded with material.

Now, there have been a number of attempts to explain this freak occurrence in the past few years, ranging from conspiracy theories, over religious prophecies, to official statements, but the source of the sound remains a mystery. As there is still so much room for speculation, it isn't surprising that there are some who attribute the noise to some kind of UFO activity, but judging from the way this phenomenon manifests, it's likely that the UFOs would have to be invisible if they were the cause. Furthermore, in the field of conspiracy theories, others suggest that the sounds are provoked by manipulations in the ionosphere, conducted by the infamous and highly mystified HAARP technology. The so-called "Project Blue Beam" is also sometimes theorized as the culprit. Then, of course, some religious folks, particularly in Christian and Muslim circles, believe that the sky trumpets are a sign of the coming apocalypse, as prophesized in the accompanying scripture of these religions.

In the channels of science, however, there have been logical explanations, although inconclusive and uncertain. While acknowledging the phenomenon, NASA said very little to shed light on the events, simply stating that these occurrences are natural and not caused by alien spaceships. They said that our planet emits such sounds and signals all of the time and due to numerous reasons, but they are usually too low in their frequency for humans to detect. This still leaves the question of why the sky trumpets are sounding off with increased intensity since less than a decade ago. What has changed so that we started hearing them so recently throughout the world?

Well, one traditional theory has to do with the Earth's mantle. It alleges that the lithosphere, the top shell layer of the planet, separates into multiple tectonic plates, which produce the sound as they grind against each other. The idea is that the sound bounces back off the upper atmosphere in a different frequency, which is more audible for the human ear. However, this theory has not been confirmed yet. One of the reasons is probably the fact that the grinding or any abrupt movement of the tectonic plates should usually produce detectable vibrations, and even tremors and quakes. And yet, the phenomena in question often occur without any earthquakes happening in the area.

The next theory takes us deeper into the Earth – much deeper. This one says that the sound is caused by some new developments in the Earth's core, which are altering the speed of our planetary mantle's movements. The pulses of energy which are ejected during certain motions and shifts in the crust are propelled upwards into the atmosphere and reflected back to Earth in the fashion I described above. All of this is said to be part of a natural process where our planet's magnetic field is having its poles inverted. This has happened in the past, and the last shift was supposed to occur around 500,000 years ago! This means that we are running behind schedule and may indeed be approaching this next pole shift.

In fact, mainstream science broadly agrees that our next polar shift has begun already or at least that there are signs of it, which greatly corroborates our theory here. The reversal of Earth's magnetic poles, many scientists agree, may have significant repercussions; life-threatening consequences as a matter of fact. The Earth's magnetic field also serves to bolster our planet's protection against harmful radioactive emissions caused by solar blasts and storms. During the process of pole shifting, which is a gradual one, the magnetic field withers and becomes fragile before it snaps into its new, reversed alignment. It is, therefore, rather obvious how this process may leave us exposed and at the mercy of our life-giving Sun. To make matters worse, it has indeed been observed by scientists that the Sun's radiation blasts have been growing more intense in the recent past and becoming more frequent since 2011. These intensifying pulses of radiation are also believed by some to be the cause of the strange sounds emitting from our atmosphere.

As more people caught on to this explanation, suppositions have cropped up that the noise may also be a form of a warning system, directed at us from the outside by extraterrestrials trying to alert us to an imminent catastrophe. Whatever explanation seems more appealing to you, the whole phenomenon stands as fascinating, no matter how you look at it. And what's perhaps the strangest aspect of this story, even more peculiar than the sky trumpets themselves, is how little attention is being given to these events by the mainstream media and the public at large.

The Hum

Yet another unexplained phenomenon in the form of a sound, the Hum has persistently baffled scientist and common folk alike since the Cold War era. The Hum manifests itself as a persistent, low-frequency sound that has been reported throughout the world by many people. Some of the most famous and widely reported instances are the Taos, Auckland, and the Bristol Hums. Its source is still to be determined with any real certainty, which is why a wide range of theories have emerged over the decades.

What makes the Hum so difficult to investigate is also the way it presents itself to observers. Namely, research and interviews in locations where it has been reported have shown that only around 2% of people are able to register the sound, while others don't notice it at all. Those who do hear it, however, usually complain that it becomes unbearable over time, leading to sleep deprivation, fatigue, headaches, and severe irritation. There have even been a couple of suicides officially tied to the stress caused by the sound as well. Based on the testimonies, the noise resembles the buzzing or humming of a machine such as a generator or an engine, or an electronic device. It also possesses a vibration of sorts, the likes of which would be a deep bass, sometimes throbbing repeatedly. Some of the sufferers have also reported that the Hum causes them to feel an actual vibration through their body.

While the descriptions given by those who experience the noise have helped reconstruct it in audio format, there have been a few claims of real recordings of the Hum, though they are often disputed. As you can see, the nature of the sound is such that it would prove very difficult to pick it up on any kind of recording device. That, as well as the fact that it's only heard by a small portion of people, has led some experts to explain the phenomenon as a case of tinnitus, which is a disorder that causes a person to hear sounds that are not physically present on the outside. However, this has been dismissed by many due to a number of factors, and the Hum is now recognized as a worldwide occurrence by scientists at large, as it has been confirmed to emanate from an outside source since the 1990s. One of the reasons for this is the fact that the hearers of the Hum also report that it stops after they move away from the location where it's present. It also appears that the Hum is a relatively modern phenomenon, taking reports and testimonies into account.

What's interesting is that people who perceive the Hum often report that it is much louder during the night, with some reporting that it doesn't occur during daytime at all. Another fairly common aspect of the sound is that it's more intense indoors, which can be explained by the isolation and the silence provided by a house or building, which shields the listener from the other sounds resonating outside.

Now, as far as conspiracy theories go, the bewildering Hum has been attributed to anything from UFO activity to government black ops, mind control experiments, and spy radio stations. An especially popular theory again concerns the HAARP experimental technology. The High-Frequency Active Auroral Research Program, or HAARP, has been the object of numerous conspiracy theories since its inception in 1993. In simplest possible terms, the purpose of this project, officially at least, is to study the ionosphere, though it can directly affect it in a few ways as well. The unusual degree of secrecy surrounding the project didn't help avert the theories either. Another possible magnet for conspiracy theories is some of the participants and funders of this project, which include parts of the US military and the Department of Defense, like the Air Force, Navy, and DARPA.

Besides the puzzling Hum, HAARP has been blamed for other things as well, such as weather control, causing earthquakes, mind control, and harming the atmosphere. It's also known that Russia and Europe operate similar facilities of their own.

The Hum has also been ascribed to machinery, oil refineries, and construction sites. Although there have been cases where these explanations proved true, such instances are a small minority. One rather peculiar explanation came from where you'd least expect it. Some researchers speculated that it was caused by no more or less than fish! There was a scientific basis to claim this, as it was believed that certain species of fish, in some of the locales where the Hum was heard, were emitting a very powerful mating call in massive numbers, allowing the frequency to reach people at greater distances. A lot of these fish were nocturnal creatures as well, which added up. These theories have since been widely dismissed, though, as it was found that many people still heard the Hum in circumstances where it would be impossible for these mating calls to reach.

While this noise is still being reported from all over the world and remains a general mystery, recent years have seen a new proposal as to what may be the cause. This theory proposes that the Hum is caused by barely noticeable seismic activity in the Earth, brought on by nothing more spectacular than ocean currents. In simpler terms, the waves at sea are causing slight inland vibrations, which are then picked up by people as distant humming. This study was done by a team of French scientists and published in the Geophysical Research Letters. It is possibly the best breakthrough we currently have trying to explain this phenomenon.

But regardless, the Hum remains generally unexplained and continues to torment those afflicted to a great extent. There are plenty of accounts by people stating that the Hum is all but ruining their lives, as it prevents them from getting a healthy, natural sleep, makes them nauseated, moody, and makes their heads hurt. Unlike our previous mystery, the Hum has been more widely reported on by many, including the mainstream media in the US and the UK, though it's been very troublesome to record the actual sound.

Thanks to many different reconstructions, and a few purported recordings, though, it is still a phenomenon that you can mainly examine on your own. Towards whichever theory you may lean, such occurrences rightfully fascinate us all.

The Tunguska event

The chances are good that some of you have already heard at least a little bit about this one. The infamous event at Tunguska in 1908 is the greatest, most destructive impact ever recorded and documented. It refers to a devastating explosion that occurred in the proximity of the Tunguska River, in the Krasnoyarsk region of Siberia, Russia. Although this incident has been covered in dozens, perhaps hundreds of scientific research papers, new theories, and speculations, some of which are rather wild, are still emerging.

There are numerous reasons as to why the event is still shrouded in a considerable amount of mystery. First of all, it happened a long time ago, when our technology, which is necessary to accurately record, study, and research, was far less advanced. It happened in a very remote area of the desolate Taigas of Siberia, reportedly causing no human deaths despite the sheer destructive power that reached and decimated over 800 square miles of forest, yielding a force equivalent of over 10 megatons – far over according to some. For comparison's sake, the most powerful nuclear weapon ever exploded by the US produced 15 megatons.

Interestingly enough, it wasn't until 1921 that the first organized expedition to the site was recorded. The tremors that were set off by the blast were registered as far as London, and yet there wasn't too much interest in investigating the supposed impact location. Keep in mind that this was closer to Russia's eastern coasts than to its European border. Could there have been secret expeditions not disclosed to the public? If so, what could they have found there? Or, were records of the initial explorations simply lost in the turbulent years that came to pass in Russia in the years after the incident? These are questions to which the answers may never be given.

Making matters even more inconclusive, there is the question of whether the Tunguska event should even be classified as an impact event. By almost all indicators, this was an airburst explosion, erupting as high as six miles above ground. This means that the object, many scientists say either an asteroid or a comet, had to disintegrate into bits before hitting the surface. Smaller objects, which enter the Earth's atmosphere more often than you'd think, do disintegrate after their entry indeed. But, it is estimated that whatever caused the destruction at Tunguska had to be between 200 and 600+ feet in diameter. It would probably take a while for an object of that size to turn to smithereens, and yet, no crater has ever been found at the site.

All of these factors have made it difficult to precisely pinpoint what happened with absolute certainty, which is why people are still theorizing, and some are still doing scientific research on the issue. There is what could be considered a consensus on the basic notion that it was a comet, an asteroid, or a meteor, but these suppositions are still to be proved beyond any doubt. Some progress has been made in 2013, where researchers found what they claim could be minuscule fragments of the cosmic object – micro-samples thereof, to be precise.

Still, this wasn't enough for many, and various theories have circulated for quite a time now. One interesting theory purported by some indicates that this explosion may have been caused by a super-weapon test conducted by Tesla, as he is known to have been working on some quite fascinating inventions in his time, many of which are objects of many conspiracy theories and speculations. And then, there are the theories revolving around UFOs and the extraterrestrials. Some of the details from the many recorded eyewitness accounts could lead one to believe a UFO was involved indeed. All manner of rumbling noise and incredible lights were reported, not just while the supposed meteor was plummeting towards Earth but also after and before the event.

There are the simple theories, which suggest that the Tunguska event was simply a UFO crash, but those are not the most interesting in this case. In particular, there was an expedition to the site in 2004, carried out by a team of researchers and one Yuri Lavbin, who led the group. He claims that his expedition found evidence or rather fragments of an alien spacecraft. These included peculiar crystals, which he said fit with each other to form some sort of device, and a block made from unknown materials, including metals. He also claimed that at least one of the crystals had a strange drawing on it. The block, which weighed around 50 kilograms, was brought in for analysis, and photos of the supposed alien materials were provided. The story was even published in a Russian newspaper. The photos are fairly inconclusive, however, and the alleged drawing could be attributed to the mere resemblance of some synthetic form, much like the famed "face" on the surface of Mars, which scientists agree is nothing but a coincidence or optical illusion.

Perhaps the strangest aspect of the story is what Lavbin claims actually happened on that morning of June 30, 1908. He doesn't simply state that it was a UFO crash, but that a UFO had, in fact, purposely collided with an incoming meteor to prevent it from obliterating us. What's unfortunate is that there has been very little in the way of results of the analysis of those materials being published, and it appears as though there hasn't been all that much effort to strengthen the theory in the years after the expedition. The story seems far-fetched as it is, and this lack of subsequent publicity does further take away its credibility. So, what could it be? Was Dr. Lavbin simply exaggerating or even making things up? Or was he swayed to stop his efforts by somebody once his information started getting out?

As always, we are left with but a taste of what the truth may or may not be. The lack of any direct and unambiguous evidence of a meteor or other natural, cosmic objects prevents the science community from reaching a definitive answer, and the usual lack of concrete signs of extraterrestrial activity puts up that other wall too. As things stand, the mysterious Tunguska event remains exactly that – a mysterious event, though with a very high profile and undeniable consequences.

Chapter 13: Alien & UFO Fun Facts

In this chapter, you will learn:

- Fun facts about aliens & UFOs
- Information you've never heard of before

After all of these theories, suppositions, conspiracies and speculations, I thought you and I deserve a bit of a break with some facts – fun facts about aliens and UFOs. Maybe you are already acquainted with some of them, perhaps they're all brand new, or maybe you're the UFO expert, and nothing about the final frontier is a mystery to you. Why don't you find out?

1. The majority of modern scientists do not consider UFOs and aliens as a real possibility, so they don't think it's even worth investigating.
2. One of the most well-known UFO religions (other than Scientology) is the Aetherius Society, which was created in 1954 by George King. He said he was appointed the Voice of Interplanetary Parliament by extraterrestrials.
3. The classic representation of the flying saucer with the dome on top was inspired by the 1958 film, Earth vs. The Flying Saucer. The dome, as well as the rotating panels, were later adapted into other movies, as well.
4. World-famous philosopher Carl Jung was of the opinion that the appearance of flying saucers represented mandalas, a reflection of the humans longing for stability in our hectic reality.
5. Area 51 is also known as "Dreamland, " and it is said that the name comes from a poem by Edgar Allan Poe.

6. The Freedom of Information Act brought documentation to prove that a number of agencies have collected and continue to collect UFO information: the Air Force, the CIA, the Defense Intelligence Agency (DIA), the NSA, the Navy, the FBI, and Army military agencies.
7. The very first photos ever taken of a UFO were in 1883, and they were taken in Zacatecas, Mexico, by Jose Bonilla, who was an astronomer.
8. The Condon report was conducted in 1968, and it was the last UFO study in the United States that received significant funding. The conclusion was that it was not worthwhile to study UFOs, but the theory in the UFO community is that the government was directly interested in dismissing ideas about the existence of UFOs.
9. The first time someone ever used the word "saucer" to describe a UFO was as early as 1878 when an American farmer spotted an unfamiliar object in the sky and said it had the shape of a saucer.
10. "Flying saucers" were investigated in Southern England in 1967, but they ended up being an intentional misleading action at the hands of some engineering students.
11. There is a passage in the Bible that some hold up as proof of UFO mentions in the Holy Book: "great cloud with fire enfolding itself, a wheel in the middle of a wheel that descended and fired lightning bolts into the earth," as described by the prophet Ezekiel.
12. Movies limited themselves to showing the types of aircraft at first, and it took until the 60s for them to show actual aliens, like in the movie The UFO Incident. In this production, we can observe the "classic" alien representation with gray skin, almond eyes, and huge heads. This image is U.S.-centric, however, as in other parts

of the world, the typical image of the alien is different. In Russia, for instance, they had small heads.
13. Carl Sagan was an astronomer who was highly skeptical about the paranormal, UFOs and alien activity, but he was deeply involved in the SETI (Search for Extraterrestrial Intelligence) project. This project is dedicated to searching space for radio signals.
14. Only 5% to 20% of UFO sightings are actually without explanation; the rest can all be dismissed as nacreous clouds, hoaxes, balloons, meteors, noctilucent clouds, aircraft, etc.
15. The U-2 flights accounted for more than 50% of the UFO sightings from the 1950s and 1960s in America.
16. UFO conspiracy theorists describe "Men in Black" as government agents hired to make sure UFO witnesses keep their mouths shut, in order to preserve the secret. They are threatening and efficient, and some believe they are themselves aliens.
17. The story of Betty and Barney Hill (recounted earlier in this book) is the first alien abduction claim back in 1961.
18. In 1991, a poll concluded that as many as 4 million people believed they had been abducted by extraterrestrials.
19. The year 1947 gave the start of the modern UFO era when Kenneth Arnold (who was a pilot) saw nine different objects in Mt. Rainer, Washington. They were deemed "flying saucers" by a reporter, and the term stuck.
20. The Atlantic Ocean is primarily known for the area called The Bermuda Triangle, where people, ships, and aircraft disappear and strange things happen. One supposition is that there is a concealed UFO base undersea and that all the

strange occurrences are because of UFOs and aliens. It is unclear whether or not they are supposed to be abductions.

21. Peru has a surprisingly high incidence for strange aerial phenomena. Due to this fact, UFOs have once again started being investigated by the Department of Investigation of Anomalous Arial Phenomena (DIFAA).
22. While up until the 1960s, people were concerned with flying saucers, after that, aliens came in front view. Claims of having talked to extraterrestrials or having visited their planets were on the rise until the 70s, when the stories turned darker, with aliens engaging in kidnapping, mutilating and other crimes, in contrast to their previously reported friendly demeanor.
23. One of the most well-known UFO stories was the one told by Harold A. Dahl in 1947. He claimed he saw them fly over Maury Island, but he admitted later that it was only a hoax. "Men in Black" were mentioned.
24. Travis Walton claimed to have been abducted in 1975 and the movie Fire in The Sky, from 1993, illustrates his story. At the beginning of the movie, it says that Walton had passed the lie detector test, but that was untrue; the test has been faked in order to create hype and publicity. The real lie detector test done by the authorities resulted in failure.
25. The period up until 1958 had the most reported sightings of flying saucers, with the stories decreasing in number after that.
26. 12,618 UFOs were supposedly spotted in the 1947-1969 period, according to the Project Blue Book. This was a UFO research agency. Out of all of those, only 107 have yet to be explained or identified.

27. A Gallup poll reports that more than 9 in 10 Americans know what a UFO is. Fewer people identified the name of Gerald Ford six months after he left office than people who identified the term UFO.
28. The term UFO first appeared in a published work in 1953 in Donald E Keyhoe's Flying Saucers from Outer Space.
29. It was common for the Soviet Union to start reporting UFO sightings in periods of secret testing of military rockets.
30. A Gallup poll found out that in 1996, more than two-thirds (71%, to be exact) of U.S. citizens were convinced that the government was hiding information about UFOs from the public.

Chapter 14: The Latest Alien and UFO News

In this chapter, you will learn:

- What the most recent alien news is
- What advancements or new discoveries have been made

Are we close to finding aliens? Not yet.

One question shows up over and over again, as technology advances and we learn more and more things about space, the universe, and the life forms it is likely to be able to sustain: are we any closer to discovering intelligent life forms? Are we going to contact aliens soon? Skeptics say never, pragmatics say we can't really tell... Stephen Hawking says not in the near future. In fact, not in the next 20 years, probably.

Early in April (April 12), Stephen Hawking was present at the Breakthrough Starshot news conference in New York. He, together with other scientists and their investor (Yuri Milner, a billionaire from Russia) talked about their project entailing sending small ships to the Alpha Centauri star system, which is neighboring ours. Milner explained that at just 20% of the speed of light, the spaceships will get to their destination in two decades and will be able to perform a series of activities that are not possible from here, like measuring magnetic fields, probing molecules of space dust, or taking close-ups.

The discussion veered to aliens and whether or not it is probable for us to establish contact or even find them. Stephen Hawking gave a disappointing if measured and honest answer and said that there is a very small probability for us to identify intelligent alien life over the next two decades. However, that is a minuscule time-frame, when we judge by space discovery standards, and he did mention that the general understanding is that just in our galaxy, there are billions (yes, with a "b") of planets that provide habitable environments, as shown by the Kepler mission. According to Hawking, that means that it's definitely likely that other life forms, or even civilizations, are to be found.

The scientist was also asked about the scenario in which we would actually encounter intelligent alien life, to which he responded that it would be best that they wouldn't find us. Why? Because, as he once reasoned, intelligent alien life may actually represent a threat to humans. Judging by that, it's in our best interest to stay hidden and lay low. Ann Druyan, the wife of Carl Sagan (astrophysicist and astronomer), expressed her bemusement that aliens are always thought to be evil and vastly technologically superior but facing the same spiritual and emotional limitations as we do.

Hawking himself was of the opinion that for all their flaws, aliens might be better than humans for the simple fact that they are different. He joked about it, referring to the current electoral campaign going on in the U.S. at the time, where a series of unlikely candidates are facing off in November.

"Wow!" explained?

Every alien aficionado probably knows the story behind the infamous "Wow!" radio signal. For decades, it stood as the most reliable proof of the existence of aliens and one of the few pieces of evidence that any kind of communication has been established. In 1977, Jerry Ehman was on the radio telescope belonging to Ohio State University, looking for alien signals. Did he actually expect to find something? I don't know, and that's something only he really knows. But what I *do* know is that he came across something that has not yet been completely figured out.

A 72-second radio wave signal was detected by the Big Ear (the telescope). It was very strong, stronger than the background noise and stronger than any signal that has ever been recorded since. Ehman printed it out and circled the signal with a short, but powerful comment: "Wow!". It turns out that the comment was well deserved because this was exactly what he was hoping for and what he was waiting for. This was a radio signal that could have been produced by an intelligent extraterrestrial life form.

The printout from that night illustrates some letters and numbers, some of them circled in red pen. These are meant to show the strength of the signal, which, as demonstrated by Ehman, went from 6 to 7 to U and then back to a lower 5. That was, indeed, a "Wow!" kind of signal. Its power is impressive precisely because no other signal of that strength has been encountered since that fateful night in 1977, which, of course, fuels rumors, stories, and conspiracy theories.

But after all those decades of radio silence, a former analyst for the U.S. Department of Defense, Antonio Paris from St. Petersburg College, thinks that he will be able to figure out what happened. He doesn't believe that it was aliens, but something else – namely, comets. Two comets, 335P/Gibbs and 266P/Christensen, were found in 2008 and 2006 so they couldn't have been thought of as the reason for the 1977 signal; no one knew they existed! That opens up a whole new set of possibilities. But a question still remains? How would these comets influence the radio signal?

1420MHz radio frequency is the key, here. Why? Because that was the band that was used and that is, according to experts, the frequency that would be used by potential intelligent life forms. If they are at least as advanced as we are and they are actively looking for similar life forms, just as we are, then we can reach the conclusion that this is the band to be on for optimal chances of contact. Now, cosmic neutral hydrogen has a natural radiation of the same frequency – 1420MHz. So this signal is not uncommon in astronomy.

This last bit of information becomes of vital importance when I tell you that the atmosphere of a comet is abundant in hydrogen. Yes, that means exactly what you think it means, and what Paris is assuming: the spectacular radio signal could have been caused by the passing of these comets. That's the bad news. The good news is that in 2017 and 2018, Comet 266P and Comet 335P will orbit through the same place again, giving scientists a chance to test this theory out. For Paris to do that, he would need a radio telescope, and they are all booked. Therefore, he is crowdfunding the $20,000 he requires to build radio antennae.

At this point, we cannot yet know what the truth is; we can only speculate, as with most things related to UFOs and alien life forms. However, this hypothesis is incredibly important, especially if it turns out to be true because it would provide an answer to a question that has been on our collective minds for decades. Of course, if this ends up being the likely explanation, that will be disappointing for all those who were holding out for a genuine extraterrestrial connection. But all hope is not lost – we will find out soon enough, and the universe is vast, after all. Anything can happen.

Best Practices and Common Mistakes

Do's

- **Keep an open mind.** This is the most important piece of advice that I can give you when it comes to this topic. I can't tell you whether to believe in the existence of aliens or not – partially because that is not a judgment call I can make and partially because I think you should be the one to decide – but I can encourage you to be open to possibilities and ideas from both sides. Evidence in either direction is a good sign, so embrace openness and willingness to change your mind or shape your understanding.

- **Do as much research as possible.** You can't base your opinion on something like this on a single source or text. It is essential that you inform yourself from as many sources as possible. Knowledge is power, and whether you find evidence to support claims of extraterrestrial presence or you discover that the most popular alien encounters were hoaxes, it is always better to be thoroughly informed on the topic before you form an opinion.

- **Seek first-hand accounts.** The fairest and easiest thing to do is look up the first-hand accounts about aliens for yourself. If you don't have the possibility to talk directly to a person who has made claims to have seen aliens, at least read or listen to interviews and stories. Being exposed to their experience is very helpful in establishing their honesty, in your own eyes.

Don'ts

- **Don't ignore evidence.** Sometimes, when the evidence doesn't fit our already-formed opinion, we dismiss it or ignore it. But no matter on which side of the issue you find yourself, evidence is evidence, and it should never be discounted, regardless if it supports your personal theory or shatters it.

- **Don't allow your opinion to stagnate.** You cannot form an opinion and stick with it, without taking in new information and developments. Information appearing from one day to another can make a world of difference and completely transform your view of things.

- Don't forget to trust your gut. The strongest believers just *know*, somewhere, deep inside, that they are right. This doesn't mean that you should not pay attention to evidence, but it does mean that you should follow your intuition when you can "smell" that something is happening.

Conclusion

After having read the book and had time to mull it over, what do you think about aliens? Do they exist or are they just a sci-fi bedtime story for adventurous kids and big Hollywood productions? If they exist, why haven't we had contact with them yet? Or did that happen and we are not being told about it? Why would NASA lie to us like that? Or maybe it's coming from the government. Is alien invasion a legitimate concern, or is it akin to the zombie apocalypse many are dreading? Maybe these are not questions we have the answers to right now, but as you saw, the information is there. Something is definitely fishy when it comes to the existence of aliens – if only we knew *what*.

These are all sound questions to ask yourself, especially if you are unsure about aliens and what you think about the issue. Contradicting statements and evidence comes up all the time, so it's difficult to form a definite opinion on the matter. Some would even say it's impossible because we do not yet have all the pieces to this profoundly mysterious puzzle. If only there were a reputable source that could present all the facts and allow you to study everything and make up your mind.

In the absence of an official and fool proof way of finding out, reading this book comes as close to finding out the truth as possible. You should be able to form an opinion, at this point. While writing this book, at no point did I ever want to influence anyone regarding the state of things. I believe that everyone has the right to be informed and form an opinion based on the evidence we are provided access to, and that is what I tried to create in this book.

I want to thank you for allowing this book to act as your guide to all things alien-related and offer you the enlightenment you are seeking. Whether you decide you believe or not, the aim of this book was to provide you with the information that will allow you to do so. Especially with a topic as sensitive and as compelling as this one, the importance of informing yourself cannot be understated.

Therefore, if you enjoyed immersing yourself in the world of UFOs, aliens and extraterrestrial encounters and letting it uncover a whole new part of the universe before your very eyes, you will be pleased to hear that the topic is far from being exhausted. There is so much that we don't know, but that can be discussed at length and considered in our quest for determining whether or not extraterrestrial life is true. You just never know what can happen, so keeping an open mind is, perhaps, one of the most valuable lessons you will have learned from this guide. I hope you found it to be a compelling, informational and entertaining read and that it helped you come closer to a resolution on the matter.

DEFINITELY THE BEST BOOK CLUB ONLINE…

"If you love books. You will <u>love</u> the Lean Stone Book Club"

*** <u>Exclusive Deals</u> That <u>*Any*</u> Book Fan Would <u>Love!</u> ***

Visit leanstonebookclub.com/join

(AND… IT'S FREE)!

CPSIA information can be obtained
at www.ICGtesting.com
Printed in the USA
FFHW021345101019
55502066-61294FF